YOUR PREGNANCY AT A GLANCE

0 - 8 WEEKS

● Pregnancy test - you can have one from the first day of a missed period, if you wish (see 'Finding out', page 21).

● Make an early appointment to see your GP if you know you're pregnant or think you may be (see 'Finding out', page 21). Begin to think about where you want your baby to be born (see **Deciding where to have your baby**, page 28). Ask about antenatal care (see **Antenatal care and antenatal classes**, page 46).

● Some mothers start to feel sick or tired around this time or have other minor physical problems for a few weeks (see 'Common minor problems', page 68).

8 -12 WEEKS

● You'll probably attend your first antenatal appointment. Appointments will usually be monthly at first (see **Antenatal care and antenatal classes**, page 46).

● Ask about your rights at work and the benefits available (see **Rights and benefits**, page 120).

● If you're on Income Support, ask your doctor or midwife for form FW8 for milk tokens (see **Rights and benefits**, page 120).

● If you don't have regular dental check-ups, make a dental appointment. Dental care is free during pregnancy

12 - 16 WEEKS

● Find out about antenatal classes if you have not already done so (see **Antenatal care and antenatal classes**, page 46).

● Begin to think about how you want to feed your baby (see **The feeding question**, page 58).

● Make sure you're wearing a good supporting bra.

● You may be offered an ultrasound scan which will show your baby moving. Some units will do a scan at 16 - 20 weeks. Your partner may like to see this too (see **Antenatal care and antenatal classes**, page 46).

● If you've been feeling sick and tired in the early weeks, you will probably start to feel better around this time.

new PREGNANCY BOOK

A complete guide to pregnancy, childbirth
and the first few weeks with a new baby

Contents

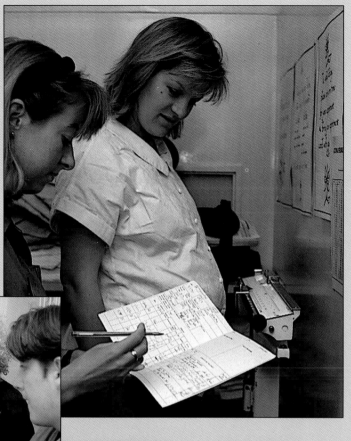

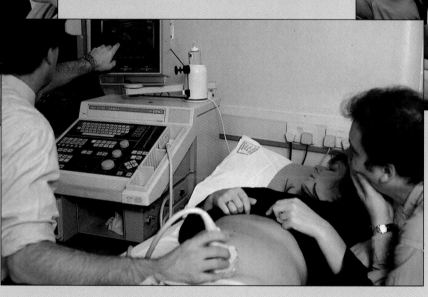

16 - 20 WEEKS

● You **may** start to feel your baby move (see **How the baby develops**, page 23).

● Your bump will probably begin to show and you'll need looser clothes.

● You may feel a new surge of energy around this time.

● Try to do your pregnancy exercises regularly (see **Your health in pregnancy**, page 8).

20 - 24 WEEKS

● Your womb will begin to enlarge more rapidly and you'll really begin to look pregnant.

● You may feel hungrier than before. Stick to a sensible balanced diet (see **Your health in pregnancy**, page 8).

● Ask your midwife if you can discuss a birth plan, if you have not already done so (see 'Birth plan', page 32).

24 - 28 WEEKS

● Get your maternity certificate, Form MAT B1 (in Northern Ireland, Form MB1), from your doctor or midwife (see **Rights and benefits**, page 120).

● Ask your midwife to let you hear your baby's heartbeat.

● If you're taking maternity leave, inform your employers in writing at least three weeks before you stop work (see **Rights and benefits**, page 120).

● If you're claiming Statutory Maternity Pay (SMP), write to your employers at least three weeks before you stop work (see **Rights and benefits**, page 120).

● If you're claiming Maternity Allowance, do so as soon as you can after you are 26 weeks pregnant (see **Rights and benefits**, page 120).

28 - 32 WEEKS

● If you're on Income Support or Family Credit, you can claim a lump sum maternity payment to help buy things for your new baby (see **Rights and benefits**, page 120).

● Think about what you need for the baby, if you have not already done so (see **What you need for the baby**, page 76).

● If you have young children, spend time getting them used to the idea of a new baby.

● Check that your shoes are comfortable. If you get tired, try to rest with your feet above the level of your heart.

● You'll probably now attend for antenatal care every fortnight.

32 - 36 WEEKS

● Make arrangements for getting to the hospital and for looking after children, if you have them.

● Pack your bag ready for the hospital.

● You'll probably be attending antenatal classes now (see **Antenatal care and antenatal classes**, page 46).

● You may be more aware of your womb tightening from time to time. These are mild contractions (see **Labour and birth**, page 79).

● You may feel quite tired. Make sure you get plenty of rest.

36 WEEKS ONWARDS

● You'll probably be attending antenatal care weekly until your baby is born.

● Make sure you have all important telephone numbers handy in case labour starts (see **Labour and birth**, page 79).

● The last few weeks can seem very long. Plan some interesting things to do to take your mind off waiting.

● Telephone your hospital or midwife if you have any worries about labour or the birth.

Introduction

Every parent is different, just as every baby is different. So there can't be many rules to having a baby. But you will find in these pages a lot of information which should help you to decide what you will do, how you will cope, and most of all how you can best enjoy both pregnancy and your baby.

Chapter 1 is about what you can do to make sure you and your baby stay healthy during your pregnancy. The book then takes you through pregnancy, birth and the first two weeks of caring for your baby. You may want to read some chapters several times, or look up specific things which interest or concern you. To find a topic quickly just look at the index at the back.

If there is anything which puzzles you, or if you need further explanation, don't hesitate to ask your doctor, midwife or health visitor.

So now what?

1 Your health in pregnancy

This chapter describes some of the things you should think about to make sure you and your baby stay healthy during pregnancy.

WHAT SHOULD YOU EAT ?

Eating healthily when you're pregnant will help your baby develop and grow and will keep you fit and well. You don't need to go on a special diet, but you do need to make sure that you eat a mixture of different foods each day in order to get all the various nutrients that you and your baby need.

You'll also need to avoid certain foods during pregnancy to be on the safe side.

- **Eat plenty of fruit and vegetables**, as these help to provide the vitamins and minerals you need, as well as fibre, which helps digestion and prevents constipation. Eat them lightly cooked in a little water or raw to get the most out of them. Frozen and tinned fruit and vegetables are good too.
- **Starchy foods like bread, potatoes, rice, pasta and breakfast cereals** are an important part of any diet and should, with vegetables, form the main part of any meal. They are satisfying, without containing too many calories, and are an important source of vitamins and fibre. Try eating wholemeal bread and wholegrain cereals when you can.
- **Lean meat, fish, eggs, cheese, beans and lentils** are all good sources of nutrients. Eat some every day.
- **Dairy products, like milk, cheese and yoghurt** are important as they contain calcium and other nutrients needed for your baby's development.

- **Try to cut down on sugar and sugary foods** like sweets, biscuits, cakes and jam, for example, and sugary drinks. Sugar contains calories without providing any of the other nutrients the body needs. It also adds to the risk of tooth decay.
- **Cut down on fat and fatty foods as well.** A little fat is essential, but most of us eat far more than we need. Fat is very high in calories and too much fat increases the risk of heart disease. Avoid fried foods, trim the fat off meat, use spreads sparingly and go easy on foods like pastry, chocolate and biscuits which contain a lot of fat. Look for low fat varieties of dairy products, for example semi-skimmed milk or skimmed milk, low fat yoghurt, and half fat hard cheese.

VITAMINS AND MINERALS

- Green, leafy vegetables, lean red meat, dried fruits and nuts contain **iron**. If you are short of iron you're likely to get very tired and may suffer from anaemia.
- Citrus fruit, tomatoes, broccoli, blackcurrants and potatoes are good sources of **vitamin C**, which you need to help you to absorb iron.
- Dairy products, fish with edible bones like sardines, bread, nuts and green vegetables are rich in **calcium** - vital for making bones and teeth.
- Margarine or oily fish (like tinned sardines) contain **vitamin D** to help you absorb calcium, but the best source of vitamin D is sunlight so try to get out for a while every day.
- Before you get pregnant and for the first 12 weeks of pregnancy, you need extra **folic acid**. This helps prevent spina bifida and other serious problems. You can get folic acid from green, leafy vegetables and from breakfast cereals and breads which have had folic acid added to them. Check the labels.

TAKE CARE WITH SOME FOODS

Besides eating a wide variety of foods, there are certain precautions you will need to take in order to safeguard your baby's well being as well as your own:

- **Make sure eggs are thoroughly cooked** until the whites and yolks are solid, to prevent the risk of salmonella food poisoning.
- **Avoid eating all types of paté and ripened soft cheese,** like brie and camembert, as well as goat and sheep milk cheese and blue-veined cheese, because of the risk of listeria infection.
- **Drink only pasteurised or UHT milk** which have had the harmful germs destroyed. If only raw or green-top milk is available, boil it before you drink.
- **Don't eat liver or liver products** - like liver paté or liver sausage - as they contain a lot of vitamin A. Too much vitamin A could harm your baby.

Vitamin supplements
Most people get the vitamins and minerals they need from the food they eat. Some people need extra, particularly those on a restricted diet. Your doctor will prescribe vitamin supplements if you need them. Don't take them without getting advice. Avoid vitamin A supplements as too much could harm your baby.

Folic acid. This vitamin is special. Folic acid tablets should be taken before you get pregnant. Take 0.4 milligrams (400 micrograms) a day until you're 12 weeks pregnant. Even if you're late starting the folic acid, still take it until you're 12 weeks pregnant.

If you're on a restricted diet, talk to your doctor, who may refer you to a dietitian. You may find it helpful to have some extra advice on how to eat healthily during pregnancy.

Have drinks which contain caffeine – coffee, tea and colas – in moderation, as there may be a slight risk that too much caffeine will affect your baby's birth weight. Try decaffeinated coffee, fruit juice or mineral water.

YOUR HEALTH IN PREGNANCY

> **Pregnancy and weight**
> Most women gain between 10 - 12.5kg (22-28lbs). Weight gain varies a great deal and depends on your weight before pregnancy. Follow these guidelines and you're unlikely to have grounds for worry. If you're concerned, talk to your midwife or GP. Excess weight gain can be difficult to lose after the birth of your baby. Remember, that too little weight gain is usually more of a worry than too much.

> **You can give up!**
> Stop completely - it's never too late. If you didn't manage it today, try again tomorrow. It might help to:
> ● **Find something to do with your hands, like knitting.**
> ● **When you feel the urge to smoke, do something else instead : phone a friend, do some exercises, read, make a drink.**
> ● **Expect it to be difficult at first and ask friends to support you.**
> ● **Reward yourself with the money you have saved.**
>
> You may need extra help: read the free Health Education Authority booklet **Stopping smoking made easier** or phone Smokers' Quitline 071 487 3000, for details of local support services.

FOR GENERAL HYGIENE
● Wash your hands before handling any food.
● Thoroughly wash all fruit and vegetables, including ready-prepared salads, before eating.
● Cook raw meat thoroughly and make sure that ready-prepared chilled meals are cooked thoroughly and are piping hot.
● Always wash your hands after handling raw meat and make sure that raw foods are stored separately from prepared foods. Otherwise there is a risk of contamination.
● Wear gloves or wash your hands thoroughly after gardening or handling soil.

Ask your doctor or clinic for a copy of **Enjoy healthy eating**, a free booklet published by the Health Education Authority.

SMOKING

When you smoke, carbon monoxide and nicotine passes into your lungs and blood stream. This means that: a) your baby gets less oxygen and cannot grow as well as it should, and b) the nicotine makes your baby's heart beat faster. If you're constantly breathing in other people's smoke it may also have a harmful effect.

If you stop smoking now :
● you're more likely to have a healthier pregnancy – and a healthier baby.
● you'll cope better with the birth.
● your baby will cope better with any birth complication.
● your baby is less likely to be born too early and have to face the additional breathing, feeding and health problems which so often go with prematurity (see page 102).
● your baby is less likely to be born underweight and have extra problems in keeping warm. Babies of mothers who smoke are, on average, 200g lighter than other babies. These babies may have problems during and after labour and are more prone to infection.
● it will be better for your baby later too. Children whose parents smoke are more likely to suffer from illnesses later on which need hospital treatment.

The sooner you stop, the better. But stopping even in the last few weeks of pregnancy can be beneficial. If any members of your household smoke, their smoke can affect you and the baby - before and after birth. They can help you and the baby by giving up now.

ALCOHOL

There is no evidence that light drinking or occasional drinking in pregnancy will harm your baby. But research shows that heavy or frequent drinking can seriously harm your baby's development. To be on the safe side, stop altogether or stick to no more than one 'unit' of alcohol once or twice a week.

If you're with friends who are drinking:
- Find a non-alcoholic drink you enjoy.
- If you drink alcohol, sip it slowly to make it last.
- If people try to pressure you into drinking, refuse politely but firmly.
- Don't binge.

If you have difficulty cutting down, talk to your doctor or midwife. Confidential help and support is available from local counselling services (look in the telephone directory or contact Alcohol Concern). See page 127 for national agencies who can help.

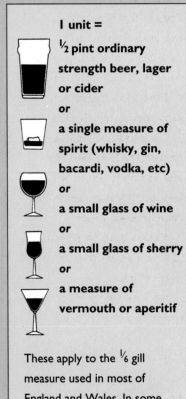

I unit =

½ pint ordinary strength beer, lager or cider

or

a single measure of spirit (whisky, gin, bacardi, vodka, etc)

or

a small glass of wine

or

a small glass of sherry

or

a measure of vermouth or aperitif

These apply to the ⅙ gill measure used in most of England and Wales. In some places, pub measures are larger than this. In Northern Ireland, a pub measure is ¼ gill – or 1½ units. In Scotland it can either be ⅙ or ¼ gill. Home measures are usually more generous.

PILLS, MEDICINES AND OTHER DRUGS

Some pills and medicine can harm the baby's health, so to be on the safe side, you should:

- assume that all medicines are dangerous until a doctor or pharmacist can tell you they are safe.
- make sure your doctor or dentist knows you're pregnant before prescribing anything or giving you treatment.
- talk to your doctor at the first possible moment if you take regular medication.

Drugs of addiction (street drugs) can harm your baby. Smoking cocaine or crack may be especially harmful because they cause a sudden drop in blood and oxygen to the placenta.

It's important to talk to your doctor or midwife straightaway so they can help refer you to a maintenance reduction programme. For more information contact SCODA (the Standing Conference on Drug Abuse) on page 127.

X-rays should be avoided in pregnancy if possible. Make sure your dentist knows you are pregnant.

PHYSICAL ACTIVITY

The more active and fit you are, the easier it will be for you to cope comfortably with your changing shape and weight - and to get back into shape again after the birth. If you feel tense after a hard day's work, physical activity is an exellent way of relaxing and it will also help you to sleep soundly.

Keep up your normal daily physical activity or exercise: sport, or dancing, or just walking to the shops and back, for as long as you feel comfortable. Don't exhaust yourself and remember that you may need to slow down as your pregnancy progresses, or if your doctor advises you to. If in doubt, consult your doctor or midwife.

- Try to keep up regular exercise at least three times a week. If you can't manage that, any amount is better than nothing.
- If you take vigorous exercise remember to start gradually and slow down comfortably.
- Avoid any strenuous exercise in hot weather.
- Drink plenty of fluids.

- If you go to exercise classes, make sure your teacher is properly qualified and knows that you're pregnant, and how far your pregnancy has progressed.

EXERCISES FOR A FITTER PREGNANCY

Every pregnant woman should try to fit these exercises into her daily routine. They will strengthen muscles to take a bigger load, make joints stronger and more flexible, improve circulation, ease backache and generally make you feel well.

Foot exercises can be done sitting or standing. They improve blood circulation, leg cramps and swollen ankles.

- Bend and stretch your feet vigorously up and down 30 times.
- Rotate your foot 8 times one way and 8 times the other way.

Pelvic rocking strengthens abdominal muscles and eases backache, which can be a problem in pregnancy.

- Kneeling on all fours, hump up your back, draw in your abdominal muscles and look at your knees.
- Now slowly relax your back (don't let it sag) and lift your head.
- Do this slowly and rhythmically 10 times, making your muscles work hard, and moving your back carefully. Only move your back as far as you can comfortably.

You can do pelvic rocking sitting on the edge of a chair with your knees apart, or standing, with your feet apart, your knees slightly bent and your hands on your hips.

Pelvic floor exercises help strengthen the muscles of the pelvic floor which come under great strain in pregnancy and childbirth. Slack pelvic muscles are one of the main reasons for the leaky bladder that some women suffer from after pregnancy. You can do this exercise anywhere: Close up your back passage as if trying to prevent a bowel movement. At the same time, draw in your vagina as if you are gripping a tampon, and your urethra as if to stop the flow of urine. Hold these muscles in as long as you can and then relax. Repeat 10 times at least five times a day.

Protect your back. As your bulge gets bigger, you may try to compensate by leaning backwards. Try to stand tall and use your abdominal muscles.

- Sit up straight with your bottom against the back of your chair. Tuck a small cushion behind your waist if you wish.
- When you pick something up, bend your knees, not your back.

MEDICAL CHECKS

RUBELLA

Rubella (another name for German measles) can seriously affect your baby's sight and hearing and cause brain and heart defects in your baby, if you catch it in the first four months of pregnancy. Most British women will have been immunised against rubella while they were at school. All children are now immunised against rubella between 12 - 15 months.

If you're not immune, and you do come into contact with rubella, tell your doctor at once. Blood tests at fortnightly intervals will show whether you have been infected and you will then be better able to think about what action to take.

SEXUALLY TRANSMITTED DISEASES

Sexually transmitted diseases (STDs) are very common and, as the early symptoms are usually mild, you may not know if you have one. However, many STDs can affect your baby's health to some extent. If you have any reason to believe that you – or your partner – could have a sexually transmitted disease which was not diagnosed before pregnancy, you should go for a check-up as soon as you can. You can ask your GP or, if you prefer, go to a hospital clinic where you will be guaranteed strict confidentiality. You can find your nearest clinic in your phone book, listed under the name of your district health authority as Genito-urinary medicine (GUM) clinic, or 'special' clinic, or the old name of VD clinic.

> **Rememember that you can get infected by HIV during pregnancy if you :**
>
> ● **have intercourse, without using a condom, with anyone who is infected.**
> ● **use injectable drugs and share equipment with an infected person.**

HIV AND AIDS

Current evidence suggests that an HIV positive mother in good health and without symptoms of the disease is unlikely to be adversely affected by pregnancy. However, about one in eight children born to HIV positive mothers, is likely to be infected. HIV positive mothers may also pass on the virus through breast milk.

If you're HIV positive, talk to your doctor about your own health and the options open to you, or contact the organisations listed on page 127 for advice and counselling.

If you suspect that you or your partner could be at risk of HIV, ask your doctor, midwife or health visitor, or go to an STD clinic (see above) for advice and counselling, before you decide whether or not

to have a blood test for HIV. If you have a test, counselling should be offered afterwards to explain the results and help you decide what to do.

HERPES

Herpes infection can be dangerous for the newborn baby. If you get recurring genital herpes, or if you or your partner develop any genital blisters or ulcers during your pregnancy, tell your doctor, midwife or obstetrician.

CHICKEN POX

Catching chicken pox could be dangerous for your baby. If you've never had chicken pox, and during your pregnancy you come into contact with a child or adult who has it, you should tell your doctor, midwife or obstetrician at once.

INHERITED CONDITIONS

Some diseases or conditions, like cystic fibrosis, haemophilia, muscular dystrophy, sickle cell disease and thalassaemia, are inherited from parents or grandparents. If you, your partner, or any relative, has a condition which you know, or suspect is inherited, or if you already have a baby with a disability, talk to your doctor about it. You may be able to have tests to check whether your baby is affected (see pages 49 and 53). Specialist advice is available from genetic counsellors.

You can talk over any of your worries with a counsellor.

ANIMALS

Cats' faeces may contain an organism which causes toxoplasmosis, a disease which can damage your baby. While you're pregnant, avoid emptying cat litter trays or, if no one else can do it, use disposable gloves. Trays should be cleaned daily and filled with boiling water for five minutes. Avoid close contact with sick cats and wear gloves when gardening - even if you don't have a cat - in case the soil is contaminated with faeces. If you do come into contact with cat faeces, wash your hands very well. Follow the general hygiene rules under 'Take care with some foods'. For further information, contact the Toxoplasmosis Trust (page 127).

Lambs and sheep can be a source of an organism called Chlamydia psittaci, which is known to cause abortion in ewes. Avoid lambing or milking ewes and all contact with newborn lambs. If you experience flu-like symptoms after coming into contact with sheep, tell your doctor.

WORK HAZARDS

If you work with chemicals, lead, X-rays, or in a job with a lot of lifting, you may be risking your health and the health of your baby. If you have any worries about this, you should talk to your doctor, your union representative or your personnel department.

If it is a known and recognised risk, it may be illegal for you to continue and your employer must offer you an alternative job, if one is available. If no job is available, your employer can dismiss you. However this would not affect your rights to maternity pay and leave (see page 122).

COPING AT WORK AND AT HOME

If you're at work during pregnancy you need to know your rights to antenatal care, leave and benefits which are set out on page 120.

You may get extremely tired, particularly in the first and last weeks of your pregnancy. Try to use your lunch break to eat and rest - not to do the shopping. If travelling in rush hour is exhausting, ask your employer if you can work slightly different hours for a time.

Don't rush home and start another job cleaning and cooking. If possible, ask your partner to take over. If you're on your own, keep housework to a minimum, and go to bed early if you can.

VDUs
Some women are concerned about reports of the effects of VDUs (visual display units on computer terminals and word processors) in pregnancy. The most recent research shows no evidence of a risk.

Safety on the move
Road accidents are among the most common causes of injury in pregnant women. To protect both you and your unborn baby, wear the diagonal strap across your body between your breasts, and the lap belt over your upper thighs. The straps should lie above and below your 'bump' - not over it.

2 Conception

To understand about conception and pregnancy, it helps to know about the male and female sexual organs. This information is useful in pregnancy too, when you want to ask questions and be clear about what you are told.

The man's sexual organs

Prostate gland

Bladder

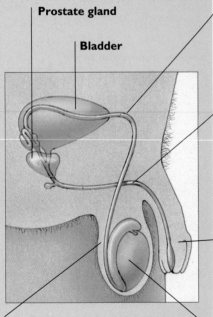

Vas deferens This tube carries sperm from the testes to the prostate and other glands. These glands add secretions which are ejaculated along with the sperm.

Urethra The urethra is a tube running down the length of the penis from the bladder, through the prostate gland to an opening at the tip of the penis. Sperm travel down the urethra to be ejaculated.

Penis The penis is made of erectile tissue. This tissue acts like a sponge and when it becomes filled with blood, the penis becomes hard and erect.

Testes There are two testes. This is where sperm are made.

Scrotum This is the bag of skin which hangs outside the body and contains the testes. It helps to keep the testes at a constant temperature, just below the temperature of the rest of the body. This is necessary for sperm to be produced. In heat, the scrotum hangs down, away from the body, to keep the testes cool. When it is cold, the scrotum draws up closer to the body for warmth.

The woman's sexual organs

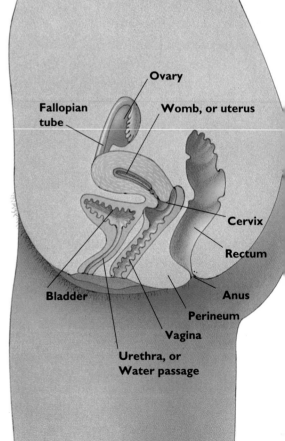

Ovary

Fallopian tube

Womb, or uterus

Cervix

Rectum

Anus

Perineum

Vagina

Bladder

Urethra, or Water passage

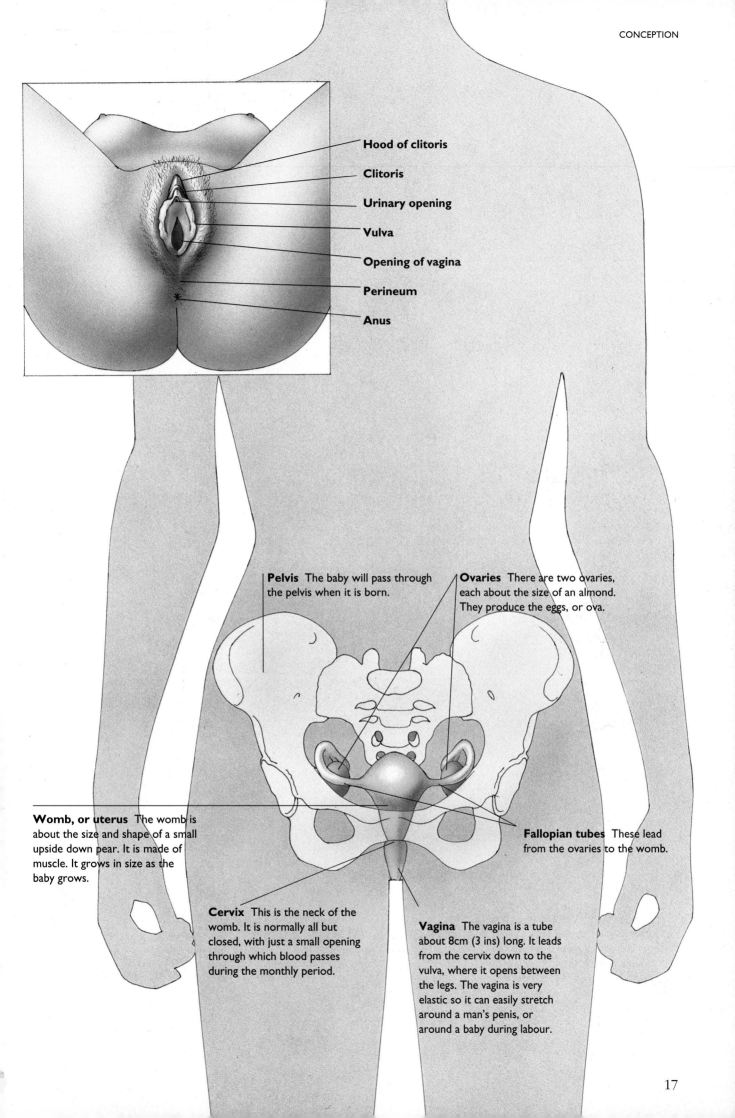

Hood of clitoris

Clitoris

Urinary opening

Vulva

Opening of vagina

Perineum

Anus

Pelvis The baby will pass through the pelvis when it is born.

Ovaries There are two ovaries, each about the size of an almond. They produce the eggs, or ova.

Womb, or uterus The womb is about the size and shape of a small upside down pear. It is made of muscle. It grows in size as the baby grows.

Fallopian tubes These lead from the ovaries to the womb.

Cervix This is the neck of the womb. It is normally all but closed, with just a small opening through which blood passes during the monthly period.

Vagina The vagina is a tube about 8cm (3 ins) long. It leads from the cervix down to the vulva, where it opens between the legs. The vagina is very elastic so it can easily stretch around a man's penis, or around a baby during labour.

17

THE WOMAN'S MONTHLY CYCLE

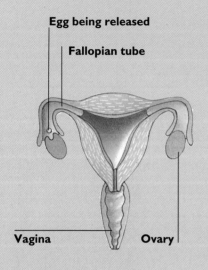

Egg being released

Fallopian tube

Vagina　**Ovary**

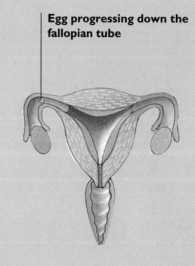

Egg progressing down the fallopian tube

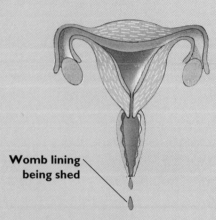

Womb lining being shed

1 Each month a ripe egg, or ovum, is released from one of the ovaries. This is called ovulation. The 'fingers' at the end of the fallopian tube help to direct the egg down into the tube. At the same time, the lining of the womb begins to thicken and the mucus in the cervix becomes thinner so that sperm can swim through it more easily.

2 The ripe egg begins to travel down the fallopian tube. It is here that it may be fertilised by a man's sperm if a couple have intercourse at this time. By now, the lining of the womb is thick enough for the egg, if it is fertilised, to be implanted in it.

3 If the egg is not fertilised by a sperm, it passes out of the body through the vagina. It is so small that it cannot be seen. The lining of the womb is also shed in the monthly period of bleeding.

CONCEPTION

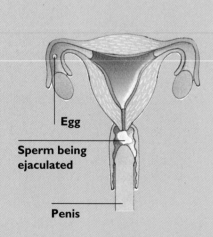

Egg

Sperm being ejaculated

Penis

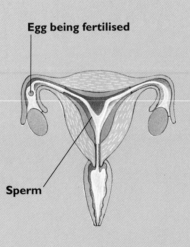

Egg being fertilised

Sperm

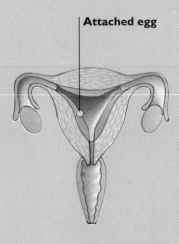

Attached egg

1 A woman is most likely to conceive just after the time she ovulates - when an egg has been released from one of her ovaries. During sexual intercourse, sperm are ejaculated from a man's penis into the woman's vagina. In one ejaculation, there may be more than 300 million sperm.

2 Most of the sperm leak out of the vagina again, but some begin to swim up through the cervix. At the time of ovulation the mucus in the cervix is thinner than usual to let the sperm pass through more easily. The sperm swim into the womb and so into the fallopian tube. One sperm may then join with the egg and fertilise it. Conception is said to have taken place.

3 During the week after fertilisation, the egg moves slowly down the fallopian tube and into the womb. It is already growing. The egg attaches itself firmly to the specially thickened womb lining.

One ripe egg, or ovum, is released from one of the woman's ovaries every month. It moves down into the fallopian tube where it may be fertilised by a man's sperm.

HORMONES

Hormones are chemicals which circulate in the blood of both men and women. They carry messages to different parts of the body, regulating certain activities and causing certain changes to take place. The female hormones, which include oestrogen and progesterone, control many of the events of the monthly cycle such as the release of the egg from the ovary and the thickening of the womb lining.

Once conception has occurred, the amount of oestrogen and progesterone increase. This causes the womb lining to build up, the blood supply to the womb and breasts to increase, and the muscles of the womb to relax to make room for the growing baby.

HEREDITY

Every normal human cell contains 46 chromosomes, except for the male sperm and female eggs. They contain 23 chromosomes each.

When the sperm fuses with the egg and fertilisation takes place, the 23 chromosomes from the father pair with the 23 from the mother, making 46 in all.

The chromosomes are tiny thread-like structures which each carry about 2,000 genes. It is the genes that determine the baby's inherited characteristics, such as hair and eye colour, blood group, height and build.

The fertilised egg contains one sex chromosome from the mother and one from the father. The sex chromosome from the mother's egg is always the same and is known as the X chromosome. But the sex chromosome from the father's sperm may be an X or Y chromosome. If the egg is fertilised by a sperm containing an X chromosome, the baby will be a girl (XX). If the sperm contains a Y chromosome, then the baby will be a boy (XY).

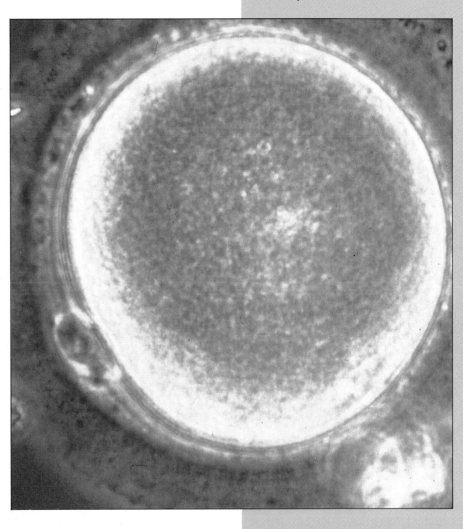

One ripe egg, or ovum, is released from one of the woman's ovaries every month. It moves down into the fallopian tube where it may be fertilised by a man's sperm

A sperm is about 1/25th of a millimetre long and has a head, neck and tail. The tail moves from side to side so that the sperm can swim up the vagina into the womb and fallopian tubes.

THE BEST TIME TO GET PREGNANT

An egg lives for about 12-24 hours after it is released from the ovary. If conception is to take place it must be fertilised within this time. Sperm can live for several days inside the woman's body. If you make love a day or so before ovulation, the sperm will have time to travel up the fallopian tubes and will be waiting when the egg is released. So the chances are highest if you make love on the day before ovulation (see chart).

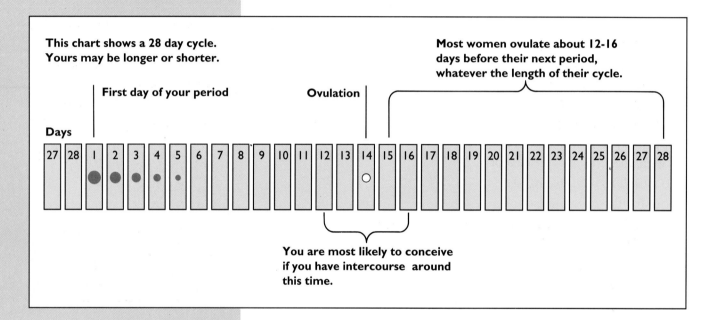

This chart shows a 28 day cycle. Yours may be longer or shorter.

Most women ovulate about 12-16 days before their next period, whatever the length of their cycle.

First day of your period

Ovulation

Days

| 27 | 28 | 1 | 2 | 3 | 4 | 5 | 6 | 7 | 8 | 9 | 10 | 11 | 12 | 13 | 14 | 15 | 16 | 17 | 18 | 19 | 20 | 21 | 22 | 23 | 24 | 25 | 26 | 27 | 28 |

You are most likely to conceive if you have intercourse around this time.

TWINS

Identical twins are the result of one fertilised egg splitting into two separate cells. Each cell grows into a baby. Because they originally came from the same cell, the babies have the same genes. They are the same sex and look very like each other.

Non-identical twins are more common. They are the result of two eggs being fertilised by two sperm at the same time. The babies may not be the same sex and will probably look no more alike than brothers and sisters.

Twins happen about once in every eighty pregnancies. A couple is more likely to have twins if there are twins in either partner's family. Triplets are much more rare and quads rarer still, although nowadays the use of drugs in the treatment of infertility has made multiple births a bit more common.

It is usually possible to find out if you are expecting twins by about the end of the second month of your pregnancy. An ultrasound scan is needed (see page 50). It is a good idea to contact support groups like TAMBA (see page 126) before the babies are born.

FINDING OUT

THE SIGNS OF PREGNANCY

The earliest and most reliable sign of pregnancy, for women who have a regular monthly cycle, is a missed period. Sometimes women who are pregnant have a very light period, losing only a little blood. *Other signs of pregnancy are:*

- **Feeling sick.** You may feel sick, or even be sick, not necessarily in the morning, but at any time.
- **Changes in your breasts.** Often the breasts become larger and feel tender, rather as they may do before a period. They may tingle. The veins may show up more and the nipples may darken and stand out.
- **Needing to pee more often.** You may find that you have to get up in the night to do so.
- **Being constipated.**
- **An increased vaginal discharge** without any soreness or irritation.
- **Feeling tired.**
- **Having a strange taste in your mouth.** Many women describe it as metallic.
- **'Going off' certain things** like tea or coffee, tobacco smoke or fatty food, for example.

Some women don't even need these signs. They just 'know' that they are pregnant.

PREGNANCY TESTS

Pregnancy tests can be carried out on a sample of urine from the first day of a missed period - that is, about two weeks after conception.

The urine best used for a pregnancy test is the first urine passed in the morning. This is when there is most pregnancy hormone in the urine. Use a clean, soap-free, well-rinsed container to collect it.

You may get pregnancy tests free from your GP or family planning clinic. Many pharmacists and most pregnancy advisory services also offer tests, usually for a small fee. You can also buy do-it-yourself pregnancy testing kits from pharmacists. They can be expensive but give you a quick result, and you can do the test in private. Follow the instructions to be sure of a reliable result.

THE RESULTS OF THE TEST

A positive test result is almost certainly correct. A negative result is less reliable. You could wait a week and try again, or go straight to your doctor.

" I thought when I first got pregnant, 'This is fantastic, it's really different, it's never happened to me before.' I expected people to be really surprised. But my sister and my family and everybody seem to have accepted it like it's an everyday occurrence. It seems a really big thing to me and yet to everybody else it's like having a cold or something."

> **See your doctor**
> **Whether or not you have had a pregnancy test, you should see your doctor as soon as you think you are pregnant. The earlier you do this the better because it is through your GP that you can make arrangements for antenatal care and your baby's birth.**
>
> **Information about the services available is given in the chapters on Deciding where to have your baby and Antenatal care and antenatal classes. It may help to look at these chapters before you talk to your doctor.**

"We'd been trying for a baby for so long and wanting it so much. Then at last I was pregnant, and suddenly I didn't want it any more. I was frightened, I think, about what we'd taken on. As soon as it was real, it was different to how we'd imagined it."

WORKING OUT WHEN YOUR BABY IS DUE

Use the chart below to work out your 'EDD' - expected date of delivery (or 'EDC' - expected date of confinement). Pick out the date of the first day of your last monthly period from the figures in black. The date your baby is due is immediately underneath it in blue. For example, if your last period started on March 12, your baby will be due around December 17. Remember that this date is no more than a rough guide.

Use this chart to work out your expected date of delivery. Pick out the date of the first day of your last monthly period from the figures in black. The date your baby is due is immediately underneath in blue.

January	1 2 3 4 5 6 7 8 9 10 11 12 13 14 15 16 17 18 19 20 21 22 23 24 25 26 27 28 29 30 31	January
October	8 9 10 11 12 13 14 15 16 17 18 19 20 21 22 23 24 25 26 27 28 29 30 31 1 2 3 4 5 6 7	**November**
February	1 2 3 4 5 6 7 8 9 10 11 12 13 14 15 16 17 18 19 20 21 22 23 24 25 26 27 28	February
November	8 9 10 11 12 13 14 15 16 17 18 19 20 21 22 23 24 25 26 27 28 29 30 1 2 3 4 5	**December**
March	1 2 3 4 5 6 7 8 9 10 11 12 13 14 15 16 17 18 19 20 21 22 23 24 25 26 27 28 29 30 31	March
December	6 7 8 9 10 11 12 13 14 15 16 17 18 19 20 21 22 23 24 25 26 27 28 29 30 31 1 2 3 4 5	**January**
April	1 2 3 4 5 6 7 8 9 10 11 12 13 14 15 16 17 18 19 20 21 22 23 24 25 26 27 28 29 30	April
January	6 7 8 9 10 11 12 13 14 15 16 17 18 19 20 21 22 23 24 25 26 27 28 29 30 31 1 2 3 4	**February**
May	1 2 3 4 5 6 7 8 9 10 11 12 13 14 15 16 17 18 19 20 21 22 23 24 25 26 27 28 29 30 31	May
February	5 6 7 8 9 10 11 12 13 14 15 16 17 18 19 20 21 22 23 24 25 26 27 28 1 2 3 4 5 6 7	**March**
June	1 2 3 4 5 6 7 8 9 10 11 12 13 14 15 16 17 18 19 20 21 22 23 24 25 26 27 28 29 30	June
March	8 9 10 11 12 13 14 15 16 17 18 19 20 21 22 23 24 25 26 27 28 29 30 31 1 2 3 4 5 6	**April**
July	1 2 3 4 5 6 7 8 9 10 11 12 13 14 15 16 17 18 19 20 21 22 23 24 25 26 27 28 29 30 31	July
April	7 8 9 10 11 12 13 14 15 16 17 18 19 20 21 22 23 24 25 26 27 28 29 30 1 2 3 4 5 6 7	**May**
August	1 2 3 4 5 6 7 8 9 10 11 12 13 14 15 16 17 18 19 20 21 22 23 24 25 26 27 28 29 30 31	August
May	8 9 10 11 12 13 14 15 16 17 18 19 20 21 22 23 24 25 26 27 28 29 30 31 1 2 3 4 5 6 7	**June**
September	1 2 3 4 5 6 7 8 9 10 11 12 13 14 15 16 17 18 19 20 21 22 23 24 25 26 27 28 29 30	September
June	8 9 10 11 12 13 14 15 16 17 18 19 20 21 22 23 24 25 26 27 28 29 30 1 2 3 4 5 6 7	**July**
October	1 2 3 4 5 6 7 8 9 10 11 12 13 14 15 16 17 18 19 20 21 22 23 24 25 26 27 28 29 30 31	October
July	8 9 10 11 12 13 14 15 16 17 18 19 20 21 22 23 24 25 26 27 28 29 30 31 1 2 3 4 5 6 7	**August**
November	1 2 3 4 5 6 7 8 9 10 11 12 13 14 15 16 17 18 19 20 21 22 23 24 25 26 27 28 29 30	November
August	8 9 10 11 12 13 14 15 16 17 18 19 20 21 22 23 24 25 26 27 28 29 30 31 1 2 3 4 5 6	**September**
December	1 2 3 4 5 6 7 8 9 10 11 12 13 14 15 16 17 18 19 20 21 22 23 24 25 26 27 28 29 30 31	December
September	7 8 9 10 11 12 13 14 15 16 17 18 19 20 21 22 23 24 25 26 27 28 29 30 1 2 3 4 5 6 7	**October**

"From the moment I found out, I felt there were two of us – me and the baby. Everything else in the world seemed less important because of what was happening inside me."

"I wasn't very pleased at first. I was a bit shocked, I think, more than anything, and it took me about three months to get used to the idea that I was pregnant. I don't think I could believe it at first."

a father: *"I wanted to do something to show I cared - cared about the baby. And there didn't seem to be anything I could do."*

KNOWING THAT YOU'RE PREGNANT

You may feel very happy or excited when you discover that you are pregnant, but you shouldn't worry if you don't. Even if you have been looking forward to pregnancy, it is not unusual for your feelings to take you by surprise. And if your pregnancy was unplanned, then you may feel quite confused.

Give yourself a little time to adjust to the idea of being pregnant. Even though you may feel rather anxious and uncertain now, this does not mean that you won't come to enjoy your pregnancy or to welcome the idea of the baby.

You may want to share the news with family and friends straightaway, or wait a while until you've sorted out how you feel. But do begin to think about your antenatal care (this is the care you'll receive leading up to the birth of your baby) and where you would like to have your baby. The earlier you begin to organise this, the more chance you will have of getting what you want.

How the baby develops

3

THE TIMING OF THE PREGNANCY

Doctors and midwives in the UK time pregnancy from the first day of a woman's last monthly period, not from conception. So what is called 'four weeks pregnant' is actually about two weeks after conception. Pregnancy normally lasts for 37-42 weeks from the first day of your last period. The average is 40 weeks.

If you're not sure about the date of your last period, then an ultrasound scan (see page 50) can give a good indication of when your baby will be due.

HOW THE BABY DEVELOPS

In the very early weeks, the developing baby is called an embryo. Then from about eight weeks onwards, it is called a fetus, meaning 'young one'.

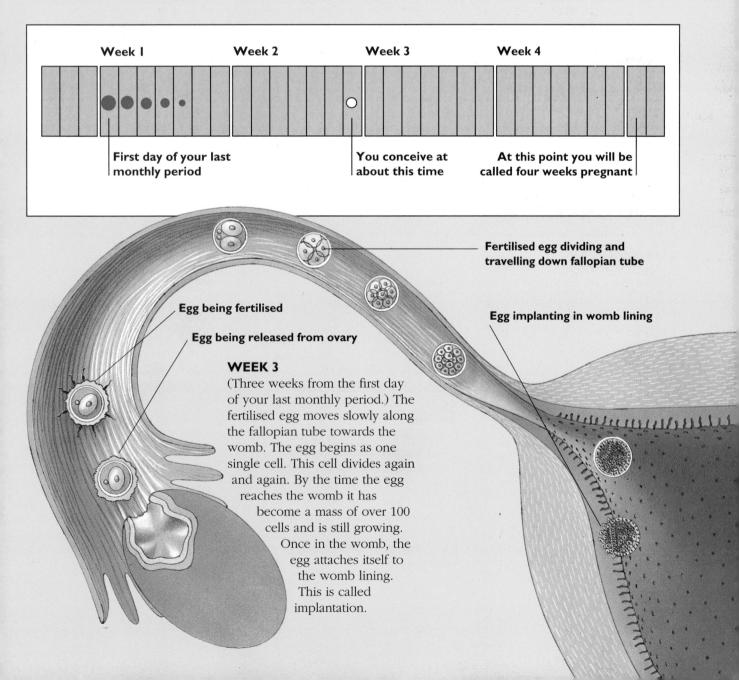

| Week 1 | Week 2 | Week 3 | Week 4 |

First day of your last monthly period

You conceive at about this time

At this point you will be called four weeks pregnant

Fertilised egg dividing and travelling down fallopian tube

Egg being fertilised

Egg being released from ovary

Egg implanting in womb lining

WEEK 3

(Three weeks from the first day of your last monthly period.) The fertilised egg moves slowly along the fallopian tube towards the womb. The egg begins as one single cell. This cell divides again and again. By the time the egg reaches the womb it has become a mass of over 100 cells and is still growing. Once in the womb, the egg attaches itself to the womb lining. This is called implantation.

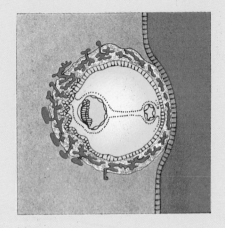

 weeks 4-5

actual size

WEEKS 4-5

The egg now settles into the womb lining. The outer cells reach out like roots to link with the mother's blood supply. The inner cells form into two, and then later into three layers. Each of these layers will grow to be different parts of the baby's body. One layer becomes the brain and nervous system, the skin, eyes and ears. Another layer becomes the lungs, stomach and gut. The third layer becomes the heart, blood, muscles and bones.

The fifth week is the time of the first missed period when most women are only just beginning to think they may be pregnant. Yet already the baby's nervous system is beginning to develop.

A groove forms in the top layer of cells. The cells fold up and round to make a hollow tube. This is called the neural tube. It will become the baby's brain and spinal cord, so the tube has a 'head end' and a 'tail end'. At the same time the heart is forming, and the baby already has some of its own blood vessels. A string of these blood vessels connect baby and mother and will become the umbilical cord.

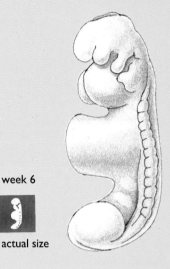

week 6

actual size

 weeks 6-7

actual size

WEEKS 6-7

There is now a large bulge where the heart is, and a bump for the head because the brain is developing. The heart begins to beat and can be seen beating on an ultrasound scan.

Dimples on the side of the head will become the ears and there are thickenings where the eyes will be. On the body, bumps are forming which will become muscles and bones. And small swellings (called 'limb buds') show where the arms and legs are growing.

At seven weeks the embryo has grown to about 8mm long from head to bottom.

WEEKS 8-9

A face is slowly forming. The eyes are more obvious and have some colour in them. There is a mouth, with a tongue.

There are now the beginnings of hands and feet, with ridges where the fingers and toes will be.

The major internal organs are all developing - the heart, brain, lungs, kidneys, liver and gut.

At nine weeks, the baby has grown to about 17mm long from head to bottom.

weeks 8-9

actual size

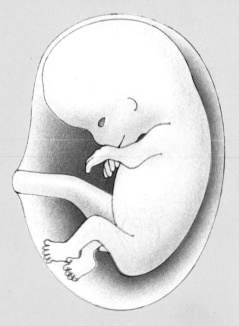

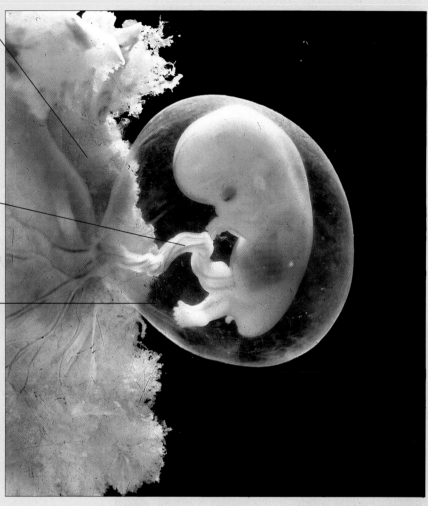

The placenta

The placenta is rooted to the lining of the womb and separates the baby's circulation from the mother's. In the placenta, oxygen and food from the mother's bloodstream pass across into the baby's bloodstream and are carried to the baby along the umbilical cord. Antibodies, giving resistance to infection, pass to the baby in the same way, but so too can alcohol, nicotine and other drugs.

The umbilical cord

The umbilical cord is the baby's life-line, the link between baby and mother. Blood circulates through the cord, carrying oxygen and food to the baby and carrying waste away again.

The amniotic sac

Inside the womb the baby floats in a bag of fluid called the amniotic sac. Before or during labour, the sac, or 'membranes', break and the fluid drains out. This is called the 'waters breaking'.

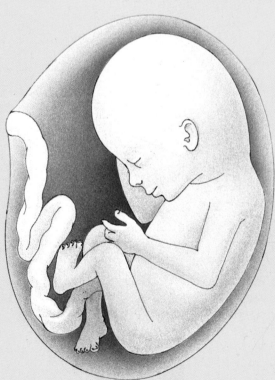

At 14 weeks the baby is about 56mm long from head to bottom. The pregnancy may be just beginning to show, although this varies a lot from woman to woman.

weeks 10-14

WEEKS 10-14

Just 12 weeks after conception, the fetus is fully formed. It has all its organs, muscles, limbs and bones. From now on it has to grow and mature.

The sex organs are now well developed. But at this early stage it is impossible to make out the baby's sex in an ultrasound scan.

The baby is already moving about, but the movements cannot yet be felt.

By about 14 weeks, the heartbeat is strong and can be heard using an ultrasound detector. The heartbeat is very fast - about twice as fast as a normal adult's heartbeat.

At 14 weeks the baby is about 56 mm long from head to bottom. The pregnancy may be just beginning to show, but this varies a lot from woman to woman.

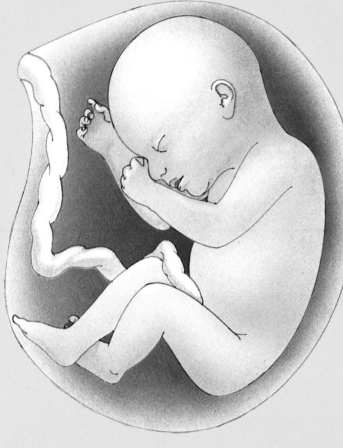

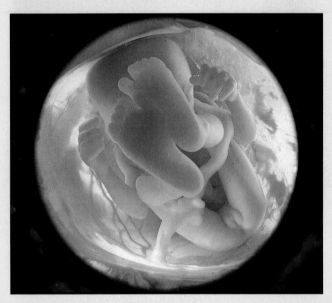

WEEKS 15-22

The baby is now growing quickly. The body grows bigger so that the head and body are more in proportion and the baby doesn't look so top heavy. The face begins to look much more human, and the hair is beginning to grow as well as eyebrows and eyelashes. The eyelids stay closed over the eyes.

The lines on the skin of the fingers are now formed, so the baby already has its own individual fingerprint. Finger and toenails are growing, and the baby has a firm hand grip.

At about 22 weeks, the baby becomes covered in a very fine, soft hair called 'lanugo'. The purpose of this isn't known, but it is thought that it may be to keep the baby at the right temperature.

The lanugo disappears before birth, though sometimes just a little is left and disappears later.

At about 16 to 22 weeks you will feel your baby move for the first time. If this is your second baby, you may feel it earlier - at about 16 to 18 weeks after conception. At first you feel a fluttering or bubbling, or a very slight shifting movement, maybe a bit like indigestion. Later you can't mistake the movements and you can even see the baby kicking about. Often you can guess which bump is a hand or a foot, and so on. Make a note of the date when you first feel your baby move and tell the doctor or midwife. The date may help check your expected date of delivery, especially if your last period is unknown and you have not had

an ultrasound test in the first half of pregnancy.

At 22 weeks, the head to bottom length is about 16cm.

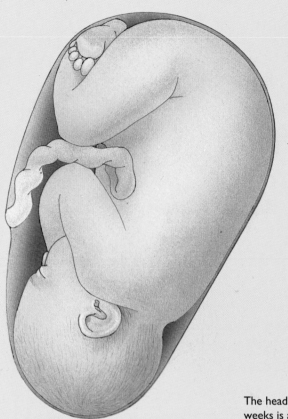

WEEKS 31-40

The baby is growing plumper so the skin, which was quite wrinkled before, is now smoother. Both the vernix and the lanugo begin to disappear.

By about 32 weeks the baby is usually lying head downwards ready for birth. Some time before birth, the head may move down into the pelvis and is said to be 'engaged'. But sometimes the baby's head does not engage until labour has started.

The head to bottom length at 30 weeks is about 24cm.

WEEKS 23-30

The baby is now moving about vigorously and responds to touch and to sound. A very loud noise close by may make it jump and kick. It is also swallowing small amounts of the amniotic fluid in which it is floating, and passing tiny amounts of urine back into the fluid. Sometimes the baby may get hiccups and you can feel the jerk of each hiccup. The baby may also begin to follow a pattern for waking and sleeping. Very often this is a different pattern from yours so when you go to bed at night, the baby wakes up and starts kicking.

The baby's heart beat can now be heard through a stethoscope. Your partner may even be able to hear it by putting an ear to your abdomen - but you have to find the right place.

The baby is now covered in a white, greasy substance called 'vernix'. It is thought that this may be to protect the baby's skin as it floats in the amniotic fluid. The vernix mostly disappears before the birth.

At 24 weeks, the baby is called 'viable'. This means that the baby is now thought to have a chance of survival if born. Most babies born before this time cannot live because their lungs and other vital organs are not well enough developed. The care that can now be given in Neonatal Units means that more and more babies born very early do survive.

At around 26 weeks the baby's eyelids open for the first time. The eyes are almost always blue or dark blue. It is not until some weeks after birth that the eyes become the colour they will stay, although some babies do have brown eyes at birth.

The head to bottom length at 30 weeks is about 24cm.

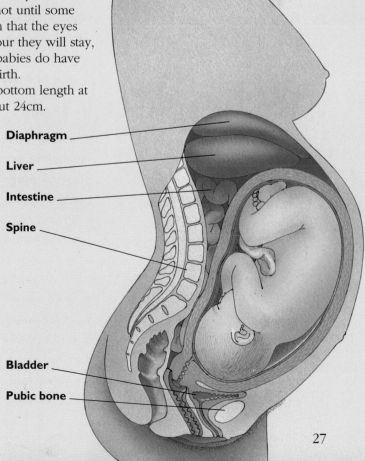

Diaphragm

Liver

Intestine

Spine

Bladder

Pubic bone

27

4 Deciding where to have your baby

Where and how you have your baby may depend to some extent on where you live but ideally you should have a choice between :

- in hospital
- in a community or GP/midwife unit
- at home

Talk things over with your doctor and midwife. They will advise you, taking into account your medical history, any difficulties with previous pregnancies and the likelihood of a straightforward delivery, but the choice is yours.

When you decide where to have the baby, you should also think about the kind of antenatal care you would like. If you have your baby at home, all your care will be either at home or at your **GP** surgery. With a **GP** delivery you will get most of your antenatal care at the surgery. With a hospital birth, care may be shared between your **GP** and the hospital. Some hospitals organise a scheme known as team midwifery. This means that a small team of midwives will care for you during your pregnancy and so you will be more likely to know the midwife who delivers your baby and helps care for you afterwards.

FINDING OUT WHAT YOUR OPTIONS ARE

Talk first to your GP. If you aren't registered with a GP, now is the time to find one. Most GPs offer some maternity care, though not all wish to be involved in the actual delivery. If you want a GP to assist in delivery, and yours is unwilling to do so, or if your GP is a man and you would feel more comfortable with a woman, you can register with another GP for your maternity care. You can continue to see your own GP for any other medical treatment.

The local supervisor of midwives (see box) or the Family Health Services Authority (FHSA) (see page 125) can give you the names of GPs with a special interest in pregnancy and childbirth.

Spend some time thinking about the options. Discuss them before you come to a decision. Remember, you can always change your mind.

IN HOSPITAL

Today most babies are born in hospital. Many hospitals try hard to meet parents' wishes and to make labour and delivery as private and special as possible. For example, many people are able to work out a birth plan with the midwife beforehand (see page 33) so that their preferences can be taken into account.

It's worth finding out in advance about how your local hospital arranges its services so that you know what to expect and have time to talk about any problems and worries beforehand. If there is more than one hospital in your district and you can choose which to go to, try to find out about the practice in each so that you can decide which will suit you best.

Use the checklist on page 31 as a guide to the sort of questions to ask. Talk to your doctor, midwife or health visitor. It's also a good idea to talk to other mothers who have recently had babies and ask them about their experiences at local hospitals. You can contact other mothers through your local branch of the National Childbirth Trust, your local Community Health Council and the Association for Improvements in the Maternity Services (AIMS) (see page 125).

COMMUNITY OR GP/MIDWIFE UNIT

This may be part of the hospital's ordinary maternity wards or a separate unit. Your baby can be delivered here by your community midwife, who has been involved in your antenatal care, and your GP (or sometimes by a hospital midwife). Some areas operate a team system, so you get to know who will deliver your baby.

You can also ask for information on your options from :
- any other **health professional**, particularly your community midwife or health visitor. Your GP or the child health clinic can put you in touch with them.
- the **local supervisor of midwives** who is also usually head of maternity services at the local maternity or district general hospital. You can get in touch through your district health authority or hospital. The addresses and telephone numbers will be in your local phone book.
- your local **Community Health Council** (see page 125).
- your local branch of the **National Childbirth Trust** (see page 125).
- the **Association for Improvements in the Maternity Services (AIMS)** (see page 125).
- friends

How to book in for a hospital delivery
Your GP will either send a letter to the hospital or give you one to take there. This is best done as early in your pregnancy as possible.

Care in a GP/Midwife or community unit can be more personal since you will usually be looked after by people you know. If the unit is in part of the main hospital, then the hospital facilities are there if they are needed. This type of unit is generally used for women for whom there is little risk of unexpected complications, and who are likely to have a normal delivery. The length of time you will remain in the unit after the birth depends on how well you and the baby are.

These units are not very common.

AT HOME

Some women want to have their babies at home. Among the reasons given are:

- They feel they will be happier and better able to cope in a place they know and with their family around them.
- If they have other young children, there will be no need to leave them to go into hospital.
- They will have more privacy.
- They will be able to relax more and will not have to fit into a hospital routine.

One or two midwives will stay with you while you're in labour and if any help is needed, will summon a doctor or send for an ambulance to get to the hospital in an emergency.

HOW TO ARRANGE FOR A HOME DELIVERY

If you want a home delivery, first talk to your GP. Most GPs advise against home deliveries for first babies, simply because it is impossible to predict how easy or difficult the birth may be. They also advise against a home delivery if it is likely for some reason that the birth will not be straightforward. So although you do have a right to a home birth, if that is what you want, obviously your first step is to find out whether or not a home birth is advisable for you.

Next you need to find out whether your own GP will be prepared to care for you during your pregnancy and a home delivery. If he or she cannot help, there may be another in the district who can. You can then register with this GP just for your maternity care (see 'Finding out what your options are' page 29). It's also a good idea to contact your local supervisor of midwives or the director of maternity services at the hospital. She will be able to arrange for a community midwife to call and discuss a home delivery.

The midwife will have an important part to play right through your pregnancy. You are most likely to see her at your antenatal check-ups and she is the first person to contact when your labour begins. She will stay with you during labour and, most often, she is the person who actually delivers your baby.

These are the kind of questions you may wish to ask about a hospital:

Would you go to the hospital antenatal clinic for all or just some of your antenatal care appointments ?

Does the antenatal clinic run an appointments system ?

Does the hospital run antenatal classes ?

Does the hospital offer the team midwifery scheme ? (This is where a woman is cared for by a small team of midwives. The woman can get to know them all, so that she will know the midwife who delivers the baby and looks after her afterwards.)

Will you be shown round the labour and postnatal wards before the birth ?

Is there a chance for you to discuss and work out a birth plan ?

Can you be seen by a woman doctor if you prefer ?

Before you try to get answers to your questions and make your decision, it will help to read the chapter Labour and birth (page 79) .

About labour and delivery

Are fathers, close relatives or friends welcome in the delivery room ?

Are they ever asked to leave the room, and why ?

Does the hospital encourage women to move around in labour and find their own position for the birth if that is what they want ?

What is the hospital policy on induction, pain relief, routine monitoring, or any other aspect of labour that concerns you ?

Afterwards

Are babies usually put to their mother's breast immediately after birth ?

What services are provided for sick babies ?

Are babies with their mothers all the time or is there a separate nursery ?

Will the hospital encourage (and help) you to feed your baby 'on demand' if this is what you want to do ?

Who will help me breastfeed my baby ?

What is the normal length of stay ?

What are visiting hours? Are there any special rules about visiting ?

BIRTH PLAN

Do you wish your partner or a chosen companion, or companions, to be with you during labour ?

Can your partner or companion remain with you if you have a Caesarean section or forceps delivery, for example ?

Is equipment such as mats, a birthing chair or beanbags available if you want it or can you bring your own ?

Are there special facilities, like special rooms or birthing pools ?

Can you choose the way your baby's heart is monitored if everything is straightforward ?

Do you prefer to be cared for and delivered by women only ?

Is it important for you to be able to move around when you're in labour ?

Is there any special position you wish to use for delivery ?

If you think you would like pain relief, which sort do you want to try? If you want to try to manage without pain relief, it's a good idea to note this in the birth plan too.

Are there other means, such as warm baths, massage or other therapies, that you would like to use to help you cope with labour ?

What do you feel about an episiotomy ?

Do you want your baby delivered straight on to your tummy or do you want your baby cleaned first ?

Do you have any feelings about the injection usually given to you after the birth to help the womb contract ?

How do you wish to feed your baby ?

Do you want your baby close to you all the time ? If you intend to breastfeed you should make a note that you want your baby close by you all the time or brought to you when hungry so that you can feed on demand.

Do you want your baby to have vitamin K, and by which route (see page 101) ?

Is there anything you feel you may need extra help with ?

Do you mind if students are present ?

Do you need an interpreter ?

Do you need a sign language interpreter ?

Do you need a special diet ?

Do you or your partner or companion have special needs that should be considered, like your partner normally used a guide dog or you use a wheelchair, for example ?

Are there special religious customs you wish to be observed ?

BIRTH PLAN

A birth plan is a record of what you would like to happen during your labour and after the birth. You may be given an opportunity to draw up a birth plan during your antenatal care. If not, ask your midwife if you can do so. Discussing a birth plan with your midwife, preferably over several meetings, will give you the chance to ask questions and find out more information. It also gives the midwife the chance to get to know you better and understand your feelings and priorities. You will probably want to think about or discuss some points more fully with your partner, or friends and relatives, before reaching a decision. And you can, of course, change your mind at any time.

There is no one, correct way to give birth. All birth plans have to be drawn up individually with your midwife. They depend not only on your own wishes, but also on your medical history and your own circumstances, and on what is available at your own hospital or unit. What may be safe and practical for one mother may not be a good idea for another.

You may sometimes put your wishes down on a special form, or have them written in your notes. At any rate, they will be available to any doctor or midwife who is caring for you during labour and afterwards. It's a good idea if you keep a copy with you as well. Of course, you should remember that if your condition or your baby's condition changes unexpectedly, the midwife or doctor may advise you to reconsider some of your wishes. It's important to remain flexible in case circumstances change.

Read the chapters **Labour and birth** and **The first few days with a new baby** before talking to your midwife, to see if there is anything you feel strongly about and might wish to include. You may find it useful to think about some of these things. You may want to take this with you to discuss with your midwife.

> **Breastfeeding**
> **If you have decided to breastfeed, your birth plan should note that you want to put your baby to your breast straight after birth. This helps to get breast-feeding started. It should also note that you do not want your baby to be given any extra formula milk feeds, as this makes breast-feeding harder.**

5 Feelings and relationships

"I think you have more extremes of emotion. You get more easily upset about things, and you can more easily get very happy about things."

"I've enjoyed it. I've enjoyed the newness of it. I've enjoyed thinking of the baby. The only thing I haven't enjoyed is getting so big."

"It's just that everybody asks you how you are all the time. Most of the time I just say 'fine' but sometimes I really feel like telling them."

From the minute you know you're pregnant, things begin to change. Your feelings change - feelings about yourself, about the baby, about your future. Your relationships change - with your partner, and also with parents and friends.

But you're still yourself, and you still have to get on with your life, whether pregnant or not. For this reason adjusting to the changes that pregnancy brings isn't always easy.

This chapter is about some of the worries that may crop up in pregnancy, and some suggestions on how to handle them. But, of course, what may be a problem for one person may not be a problem for another. And what is helpful advice for some people may not be right for you. So take from these pages what you find useful, and don't bother about the rest.

FEELINGS

When you're pregnant it can sometimes seem as though you are not allowed to have other feelings as well. People expect you to be looking forward to the baby, to be excited and to 'bloom' all the time. You, yourself, may think that this is the way you ought to be. In fact, just like any other nine months in your life, you're likely to have times when you feel low. And pregnancy does bring extra reasons for feeling worried or down, just as it brings many reasons for happiness.

Hormonal changes taking place in your body may be partly responsible for the tiredness and nausea that some women feel in the early months, and for some of the emotional upsets which can happen. You may find you cry more easily, lose your temper more, and so on. Of course, there are many other reasons why you may feel rather down. You may have money worries or worries about work or where you are going to live. You may be anxious about whether you will cope as a parent - or about whether you're really ready to be a parent at all. And many of these anxieties may be shared by your partner or family as well.

BLOOMING MOTHERS LTD.

SALE

SO BLOOMIN WHAT!

34

Talking about your feelings to your partner, or to someone who is close to you, is often a relief and can help you get things in proportion. It may help your partner too. Making sure you keep yourself well and get plenty of sleep will also help. Anyone who is tired and run down is likely to feel rather low, whether they are pregnant or not. And don't let the pregnancy take over your life. Keep on doing all the things you enjoy. Although it's normal to have some worries while you are pregnant and to feel a bit down from time to time, it's a real cause for concern if you're feeling depressed for most of the time. Whatever the reason for your unhappiness, or even if there doesn't seem to be any reason at all, explain how you feel to your doctor, midwife or health visitor. Make sure they understand that you're talking about something more than just feeling low.

WORRYING ABOUT THE BIRTH

One worry that a lot of women have in pregnancy is whether labour and birth will be painful and how they will cope. It is difficult to imagine what a contraction might be like and no one can tell you - though many will try. However, factual information about the options open to you can help you to feel more confident and more in control.

Begin by reading the chapter on labour and birth with your partner, or a friend or relative who will be with you for the birth, if possible. Ask your doctor or midwife for any further information. Antenatal classes will also help to prepare you for labour and the birth (see page 56).

Think about the sort of labour and birth you would like to have. You will probably have an opportunity to discuss this in more detail with your midwife and to draw up a birth plan during the later months of pregnancy (see page 33).

Talk to your partner too, or to someone close to you, and particularly to the person who will be with you in labour. Remember they may be anxious too. Together, you can then work out ways in which to cope.

"It frightens me, wondering what I've got to go through. People say different things, you know, so you don't know what to think."

"I loved every minute of being pregnant and went through a wonderful experience with labour."

"I think it's a lot to do with mind over matter. I think the thing to do is to just try and relax and not be frightened. I mean, it's happened to thousands and millions of people before you."

"I'll just take it as it comes. I remember I used to hate going to the dentist. I'd sit outside in the waiting room and feel sick with fear. Just with nerves. I went in one time and it hurt a bit, having the injection, but it was nothing compared to how I'd felt thinking about it outside. After that, I swore I'd never worry about things before they happen. I don't think about what'll happen at the dentist, and I don't think about what'll happen in labour."

"I'm looking forward to it, even though there may be pain. What comes out of it is good anyway."

WORRYING ABOUT ABNORMALITY

"I want to know if it's alright. I think that's always at the back of your mind - you don't know whether it's alright. It's a worry that's always there."

" I feel guilty at times. It's not just worrying about what you do and whether it will damage the baby. Sometimes I feel I just haven't thought about the baby, cared about it enough. I ought to be loving it more."

"You hear such a lot and read such a lot in the newspapers - about spina bifida and backward children and all that. You can't help but wonder about your own."

" Now that I've felt it move and I've heard the heartbeat, I feel happier. Early on we worried much more."

Everyone worries at some time that there may be something wrong with their baby. Some people find that talking openly about their fears helps them to cope. Others prefer not to dwell on the possibility of something being wrong.

Some women do find it hard to control their worry because they are convinced that if something does go wrong it will be their fault. But while you can increase your baby's chances of being born healthy by eating well and by not smoking, for example (see pages 8 - 10), you can't cut out the risk entirely. There are certain problems which cannot be prevented, either because the causes are not known or they are beyond anyone's control.

It may reassure you to know that 97% of babies born in the UK are normal, although some of these may have birthmarks or some other small variations. A further 1% of babies will be born with abnormalities that can be partly or completely corrected. About 2% however, will suffer from some more severe disability. Regular antenatal care and careful observation during labour help so that action can be taken if necessary.

If you are particularly concerned, perhaps because someone in your family has a disability, or because someone you know has had a difficult birth, or even if you just feel very anxious, talk to your doctor or midwife as soon as possible. They may be able to reassure you or offer you helpful information about tests which can be done in pregnancy (see pages 49 and 51).

COUPLES

Pregnancy is bound to bring about some quite big changes in a couple's relationship, especially if this is your first baby. For some people these changes happen easily, others find it harder to change. Everybody is different.

It's quite common for couples to find themselves having arguments every now and then during pregnancy, however much they are looking forward to the baby. Some of these may be nothing to do with the pregnancy, but others may be caused by one or other partner feeling worried about the future and how they are going to cope.

Perhaps the important thing to realise is that during pregnancy there are understandable reasons for the odd difficulty between you and also good reasons for feeling closer and more loving.

One practical question you will need to discuss is how you will cope with labour and whether your partner will be there. Very many fathers do want to be present at their baby's birth. The chapter on **Labour and birth** gives some suggestions on ways in which fathers can help and what it can mean to them to share this experience.

"You've got a bond between you. It's something that belongs to both of you."

"Sometimes it draws us together and sometimes it sets us apart. When we first found out about the baby, we were on edge. We snapped at each other a lot. Then it got better. We really wanted each other and we were really looking forward to the baby coming. It's up and down."

SEX IN PREGNANCY

Many people worry about whether it is safe to have sex during pregnancy. There is no physical reason why you shouldn't continue to have sexual intercourse right through a normal pregnancy, if you wish. It doesn't harm the baby because the penis cannot penetrate beyond the vagina. The muscles of the cervix and a plug of mucus, specially formed in pregnancy, seal off the womb completely.

Later in pregnancy an orgasm, or even sexual intercourse itself, can set off contractions (known as Braxton Hicks' contractions, see page 80). You will feel the muscles of your womb go hard. There is no need for alarm this is perfectly normal. If it feels uncomfortable, just lie quietly till the contractions pass.

If you have had a previous miscarriage, ask your doctor for advice. Many doctors think that it is safest not to have intercourse in the early months of pregnancy if you have already had a miscarriage. Your doctor will also probably advise you to avoid intercourse if you have heavy bleeding in pregnancy, and you should definitely not have intercourse once the waters have broken (see page 80).

While sex is safe for most couples in pregnancy, it may not be all that easy. You will probably need to find different positions. This can be a time to explore and experiment together. The man on top can become very uncomfortable for the woman quite early in pregnancy, not just because of the baby, but because of tender

breasts as well. It can also be uncomfortable if the man's penis penetrates too deeply. So it may be better to lie on your sides, either facing or with the man behind. Many people find the woman on top is best.

There are some couples too, who may simply feel that they don't want to have intercourse during pregnancy. They prefer to find other ways of being loving or of making love. It's important to talk about your feelings to each other.

FAMILIES AND FRIENDS

In some ways pregnancy is very private, just to do with you and your partner, but there may be a lot of people around you who are also interested and concerned about your baby - parents, sisters, brothers, friends.

People can offer a great deal of help in all sorts of ways and you will probably be very glad of their interest and their support. But sometimes, it can feel as if you're being taken over. If so, it can help everyone if you explain gently that there are some decisions that only you can take and some things that you prefer to do on your own.

You may also find that being pregnant puts you on the receiving end of a lot of advice - and perhaps a bit of criticism too. Sometimes the advice is helpful, sometimes not. Sometimes the criticism can really hurt. The important thing is to hold on to what you feel is right. After all, it is your pregnancy and your baby.

WORK

If you enjoy your work and the company of those you work with, you may have rather mixed feelings when the time comes to stop work before your baby is born. Try to make the most of these few weeks to enjoy doing the things you want to do at your own pace. It is also a good opportunity to make some new friends. You may meet other mothers at your antenatal classes (see page 56), or you may get to know more people living close by, now you have more time to stop and chat.

You may have decided that you are going to spend some time at home with your baby or you may be planning to return to work, either full or part time, fairly soon after the birth. If you know that you will be going back to work, or even if you think you might be, you will need to start thinking about who will look after your baby well in advance. It is not always easy to find a satisfactory childcare arrangement, and it may take you some time.

Any decision you make about childcare will be limited both by your income and the kind of facilities available locally. You may be lucky enough to have a relative willing to provide care. If not, you should contact your council social services department for a list of registered childminders and nurseries. Few nurseries take babies and prices are usually high. You may also want to consider organising care in your own home, either on your own, or sharing with other parents. Care in your own home does not need to be registered but you should satisfy yourself that your carer is experienced and trained to care for babies. Contact the Childminding Association or Working for Childcare (see page 127) for more information.

"There's the feeling that you're being looked after. Not just by your husband and your parents and the hospital, but by your friends, by everybody. They're there behind you. I suppose they're wrapping me up in cotton wool, but it's still a nice feeling."

"My mother starts telling me 'You must have this for the baby, you must have that', and trying to tell me what I should do. And bringing things like nappy pins and saying 'I didn't think you'd remember to get them.' It's irritating."

"We seem to have got a lot closer. We often sit and talk and my mum remembers when I was tiny."

"It's no good listening to other people. They only tell you about themselves, about what happened to them. They tell you the bad parts, too, not the good."

COPING ALONE

"The baby's dad has gone. He wanted the baby at first but when things started to happen he didn't like it, so he's gone. But my mum has been to all my antenatal classes with me and everything, so she knows what's going on."

"Sometimes I feel really low and think, 'Oh God, I'm only 18 and it's for the rest of my life. every time I go out I've got to get a baby sitter and things.' "

"I talked to the hospital social worker about things and she told me all about managing on my own."

If you're pregnant and on your own it's even more important that there are people with whom you can share your feelings and who can offer you support. Sorting out problems, whether personal or medical, is often difficult when you are by yourself, and it's better to find someone to talk to rather than to let things get you down.

You may find it encouraging to meet other mothers who have also gone through pregnancy on their own. Gingerbread (see page 126) is a self-help organisation for one-parent families which has a network of local groups, and which can offer you information and advice. They will be able to put you in touch with other mothers in a similar situation if you wish.

If money is an immediate concern, read the chapter **Rights and benefits** for information on what you can claim and your employment rights. Your local social security office, the DSS Freeline or local citizens advice bureau will be able to give you more advice.

If you have housing problems, contact your local citizens advice bureau or your local housing advice centre. Ask for the address from your local authority at the town hall.

The National Council for One Parent Families can also supply information on a range of topics from benefits to maintenance (see page 126). There may be a local support group in your area. Ask your health visitor.

Don't feel that, just because you don't have a partner, you have to go to antenatal visits and cope with labour on your own. You have just as much right as anyone else to be accompanied by the person you chose - a friend, sister or perhaps your mother. Involve your 'labour partner' in birth classes if you can and let her know what you want from her.

Think about how you will manage after the birth. Will there be people around to help and support you? If there is no one who can give you support it might help to discuss your situation with a social worker. Your doctor or hospital can refer you, or you can contact the social services department of your local council direct.

If you're considering adoption or fostering you should discuss this with a social worker.

Mainly for men

6

YOUR FEELINGS ABOUT PREGNANCY

Some pregnancies have been planned for months or years. Some come as a shock. Either way, you'll probably feel pretty mixed up. A baby means new responsibilities which, whatever your age, you may feel unready for.

Your partner may have similar feelings. It's normal for both of you to feel like this. Your first pregnancy is a very important event. It will change your life and change can be frightening even if it's something you've been looking forward to.

Money problems may be nagging at you: the loss of an income for a while, extra expenses for the baby and, if your partner returns to work, the cost of childcare. You may be worrying that your home isn't right or that you'll feel obliged to stay in a job you don't like. (It might help to look at the benefits section at the back of the book and start planning ahead.)

a father: *"It was a shock at first, but now I'm getting used to the idea. We didn't plan it, but there's no problem with that. If it had been three years ago, when we first started living together, obviously it would have been a lot worse financially. That's the main factor."*

a father: *"When the test was positive, I felt really excited, on a real high. We couldn't wait to tell everyone."*

HEY – THERE IS SomeTHiNg iN THERE!

a father: *"She became very absorbed in her own body, separate. I felt lonely and frightened of not doing the right thing."*

a father: *"My worries are to do with making sure that she's happy and comfortable and that."*

a father: *"My wife one day couldn't stand the smell of me. I tried every different kind of soap, but it made no difference. In the end I asked the doctor about it."*

a father: *"From time to time I became angry. She was complaining too much, but millions of women become pregnant don't they?"*

a father: *"I am happy to be involved. I want to know what she has to do. I like to feel involved, contributing to this, not just starting it."*

Some men feel left out. Your partner's attention will be on what's happening inside her and she may want you to pay a lot more attention to her needs than usual. You may not have realised how much you relied on her to make you feel cared for and now that her attention is elsewhere you may feel quite lonely.

Your loneliness may be increased if your partner doesn't want to make love, although some women find sex more enjoyable than ever. It varies from person to person. There's no medical reason to avoid sex but keep in mind:

- her breasts in the early weeks may be extremely painful.
- if there's any bleeding or pain avoid intercourse (and consult your doctor).
- make sure your partner is comfortable - you may need to try different positions as pregnancy progresses.

If she's not interested in sex, try to find other ways of being close - but do talk about it. If she feels that you're trying to persuade her to do something she doesn't want, she may withdraw completely leaving both of you lonely.

Some men find it hard to make love during pregnancy. They feel strange doing it with 'someone else there' or may find their partner's changing shape disturbing. This is one situation when it helps to be careful what you say. Your partner may well feel uneasy about her changing body and may be very hurt if she thinks that you don't like it either.

TALK ABOUT IT

Confide in friends who are already fathers and will know what you're going through. You may want to protect your partner from your worries but she will almost certainly sense your concern. The more you keep it to yourself the more she'll feel that you're moving away from her - just when she badly needs you to be there. If you're giving her the support she needs, then there's no need to leave your feelings out of the picture.

PHYSICAL FEELINGS

Believe it or not, men can get symptoms of pregnancy too! The most commonly reported ones are sleeplessness, indigestion and nausea. They are probably caused by stress, but no less uncomfortable for that.

SUPPORTING YOUR PARTNER

Something amazing is happening inside your partner's body. The closer you can get to her the more you'll be able to share this experience. At times closeness will seem impossible.

In the early weeks she may be prickly and irritable about the slightest things. Certain smells and tastes may make her nauseous. She may want only to sleep.

In the middle months you'll probably find that much of her energy returns and she may resent being treated 'like china'.

Towards the end the weight of the baby may drag her down. The tiredness and irritability of the early weeks often returns and she may start feeling quite frightened of the birth and be lonely without the company of friends at work.

If your partner is anxious encourage her to talk about it. Many women are more used to listening than being listened to, so it may take a while before she feels able to open up. Be patient, the better you can learn to support each other now, the stronger your relationship will be when the baby arrives.

PRACTICAL SUPPORT

Your partner may be used to doing most of the housework as well as going out to work. If she continues to do all this work she'll tire herself out. Now is the time to start sharing the housework. There are two areas where you can really help:

- cooking - in the early months the smell may put her off and if you cook she's more likely to eat what she needs.
- carrying heavy shopping can put too much strain on her back so try to do shopping together.

A FRIEND IN NEED

Pregnancy can be frightening so it will help if she knows that she's not alone. Start by reading the rest of this book with her so that you're both well informed. Some of the basic health advice is just as important for you as it is for her.

- Good eating is much easier if you're doing it together so read page 8 and start picking up the food habits you'll want to pass on to your child.
- A smokey home is dangerous for babies. Read page 10 on how to stop.
- Go with her to the doctor if she's worried, or be sure to talk it through when she gets home.
- Be there when she has her 16 week scan (see page 50) and see your baby on the screen.
- If she needs to have extra tests (see page 51) your support is specially important.
- Find out about antenatal classes for couples, or fathers' evenings at the hospital (see page 56). The more you know about labour the more you'll be able to help.
- Most men stay with their partners during labour but it's important that you're both happy about it. Make your decision together.

a father: *"A lot of men don't like to ask questions. That's one of the things that causes problems, that some men won't even ask their girlfriends questions. Some don't want to go to the scan or see their baby being born. I love it. It's going to be brilliant."*

a father: *"I'm pretty scared about going. I'm a bit of a wimp. I've never been to hospital in my life, so going through the screaming will be hard, But I suppose it will be an amazing experience because it's your own partner that's going through it."*

> **The birth –
> being prepared**
> A check list for the final weeks.
> - **Make sure your partner can contact you at all times.**
> - **Decide how you'll get to the hospital (if you're having a hospital birth).**
> - **If you're using your own car, makes sure it works and do a trial run to see how long it takes.**
> - **Remember to pack a bag for yourself including: snacks, a camera and film, change for the telephone.**

a father: *"I went home tired and anxious about the future. It didn't seem like the greatest moment in my life. I was just glad it was over."*

- Talk about what you both expect in labour (see page 33).
- Talk about the birth plan, if she has filled one in with the midwife, so that you understand the help that she would like from you.
- During labour she'll be far too involved with what's happening inside to pay much attention to the people around her. You can be her guide and interpreter.

a father: "Sundays are great. I just lie about with this little baby in my arms."

a father: "I have her to myself from 5 or 6am until I go to work. It's the best time with nobody else interfering."

a father: "I was expected to support her but nobody was supporting me. Nobody said to me 'how do you feel?' so I just got into bad moods and sulked. It would have been better to talk about how I was really feeling than pretend everything was fine and then blow up."

BECOMING A FATHER

Watching your baby coming into the world is the most incredible experience. The midwives will give you the baby to hold. Some men feel afraid of hurting such a tiny creature. Don't be. Hold the baby close to your body. Feel the softness of the head against your cheek. Cry if you want to. Afterwards, sleep if you can. You need to recover from the birth too and, when the baby comes home, you can expect broken nights for some time to come.

BRINGING THEM HOME
There was a time when relations would rally round so that a new mother needed only to rest and feed her baby for the first month or more. Now she may only have you. If you can be home from work for a week or so use it to make sure she gets as much rest as possible.

- Don't let too many visitors exhaust her.
- Encourage her to take a proper rest every day while you mind the baby.

- Take over the housework but don't try to keep the house spotless and tidy. No one will expect it.
- Use this time to do as much as you can for the baby. Learn to bath and change nappies. If you use bottles find out how they are prepared (see page 66) and share the feeding. The more you learn now, the closer you will feel to your child and the easier it will become. Enjoy cuddling your new baby.
- When you go back to work you may have to make up for her lost earnings but keep overtime to a minimum. You can't learn to be a father at work.
- Be considerate about sex. It may take many weeks before she stops feeling sore. Find other ways of being loving until she feels ready for it.

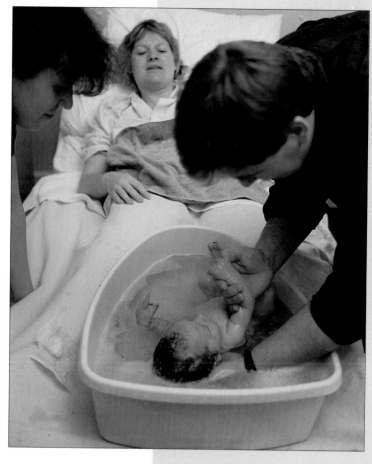

FEELING LOW

Some mothers become depressed and need a lot of extra support, both practical and emotional (see 'Postnatal depression', page 107). You may also get depressed. Your partner is facing the biggest changes but that doesn't mean that you should ignore your own feelings. You need support too. Keep talking and listening to each other, talk to friends too, and be patient - life will get easier in time.

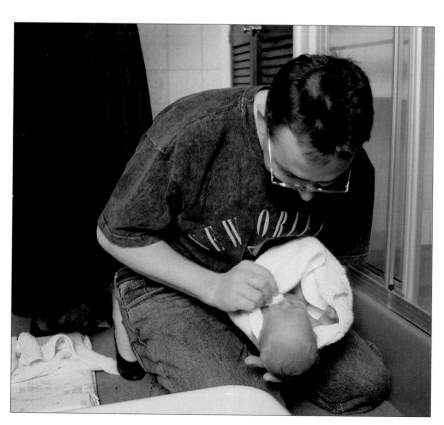

7 Antenatal care and antenatal classes

Throughout your pregnancy you will have regular care, either at a hospital antenatal clinic, or with your own GP or community midwife. This is to make sure that you and the baby are fit and well, to check that the baby is developing properly, and as far as possible, to prevent anything going wrong, either during your pregnancy or when you go into labour. This is the time to get answers to any questions, or worries and discuss plans for your baby's birth. Where you go for your antenatal care depends on where you decide to have your baby.

THE FIRST VISIT

Most women have their first, and longest, antenatal check-up around the 8th to 12th week of pregnancy. The earlier you go the better.

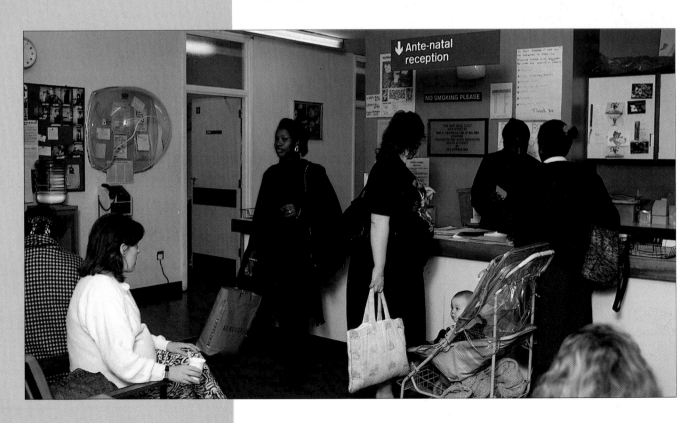

QUESTIONS

You can expect a lot of questions on your health, on any illnesses and operations you have had, and on any previous pregnancies or miscarriages. You will be asked for any information you have on your own family and your partner's family - whether there are twins on either side or any inherited illness, for example. You will also be asked about your ethnic origin. This is because certain inherited conditions that need attention in early pregnancy are more common in some ethnic groups. There may also be questions about your work and your partner's work and what kind of accommodation you live in, to see if there is anything about your circumstances that might affect your pregnancy.

All this information will help to build up a picture of you and your pregnancy so that any special risks can be spotted and support provided.

The doctor or midwife will want to know the date of the first day of your last period, to work out when the baby is due. You will probably want to ask a lot of questions yourself. This is a good opportunity. It often helps if you can write down what you want to say in advance, as it's easy to forget once you are there, and it's important to find out what you want to know and to express your own feelings and preferences.

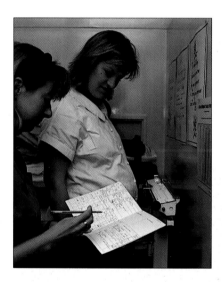

WEIGHT

You'll be weighed. From now on, your weight gain will probably be checked regularly, although not all hospitals do this. Most women put on between 10 - 12.5 kilos (22 - 28lbs) in pregnancy, most of it after the 20th week. Your ideal weight depends on your weight before pregnancy.

HEIGHT

Your height will also be measured on the first visit because it is a rough guide to the size of your pelvis. Some small women have small pelvises and may need to discuss their baby's delivery with their midwife or doctor.

If you're going to have your baby in hospital, your GP will write or give you a letter for the hospital. You will then be invited either to an antenatal clinic at the hospital, where you will see a hospital doctor and hospital midwife, or to your own GP or community midwife for most of your check-ups and to the hospital antenatal clinic for others. This is called 'shared care'. Your antenatal care is shared by the hospital and your GP and midwife.

If you're going to have the baby in a community or GP/midwife unit or at home, then you will probably go to your own GP and community midwife for most of your antenatal care. You may need to visit the hospital for an initial assessment and perhaps for an ultrasound scan or for special tests. Sometimes your midwife may visit you at home.

Remember that if you're working you have the right to paid time off for your antenatal care (see p 122).

Tests

A number of tests will be carried out at your first visit. Some of these will be repeated at later visits. If you have any questions about the reasons for these tests or about the results, or if you want any further explanations, be sure to ask your doctor or midwife.

GENERAL PHYSICAL EXAMINATION

The doctor will check your heart and lungs and make sure your general health is good.

URINE

You will be asked to give a sample of urine each time you visit. This will be checked for a number of things including:

- **Sugar** Pregnant women may have sugar in their urine from time to time, but if it is found repeatedly, you will be checked for diabetes. Some women develop a type of diabetes in pregnancy known as 'gestational diabetes' which must be controlled during pregnancy usually by a change of diet and, possibly, insulin. The condition usually disappears once the baby is born.
- **Protein** Protein in your urine may show that there is an infection that needs to be treated. It may also be a sign of pregnancy-induced hypertension (see page 75).

BLOOD PRESSURE

Your blood pressure will be taken at every antenatal visit. High blood pressure later in pregnancy can endanger you and the baby (see page 75).

BLOOD TESTS

You will be asked for your permission to take a blood sample for testing. *This is to check:*

- **your blood group.**
- **whether your blood is rhesus negative or positive** A few mothers are rhesus negative. This is not a worry for the first baby. Some rhesus negative mothers will need an injection after the birth of their first baby to protect their next baby from anaemia.

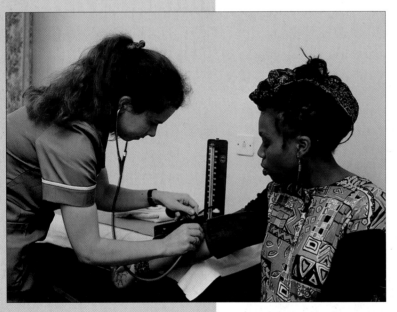

- **whether you are anaemic** If you are, you will probably be given iron and folic acid tablets to take. Anaemia makes you tired and less able to cope with losing blood - at delivery, for example.
- **your immunity to rubella (German measles).** If you get rubella in early pregnancy, it can seriously damage your unborn baby. If you are not immune to rubella, blood tests every two weeks will show whether you have been infected. If so, you'll be offered the option of ending your pregnancy.
- **for syphilis** It is vital to detect and treat any woman who has this sexually transmitted infection as early as possible.
- **for hepatitis B** a kind of liver disease which may infect the baby unless special care is taken.

Hepatitis B is a serious liver disease. You can get it by having sex with someone with hepatitis, or by injecting drugs and sharing needles with an infected person. If you're pregnant, your baby may also get it. Most children who get hepatitis around the time of birth carry the virus for life.

HIV BLOOD TEST

HIV is the virus that causes AIDS. You won't be tested routinely for HIV infection, but some hospitals are carrying out anonymous testing as part of a survey to try and find out just how widespread HIV is in the population. If your hospital is one of these, then leaflets and posters explaining the survey should be given to you.

Anonymous testing involves testing some of the blood from the routine checks described above, for HIV antibodies. But the blood sample is not labelled with your name, so it is impossible for either you, or the staff, to know the results of the test. You can decide not to be included in the survey if you wish. You can be sure that the survey will not affect your antenatal care in any way. If you think that you may have been at risk of getting HIV, ask your doctor or midwife for the opportunity to discuss HIV testing and counselling. If you're HIV positive, you can talk to someone at Positively Women, an organisation concerned with women and HIV and AIDS (see page 127).

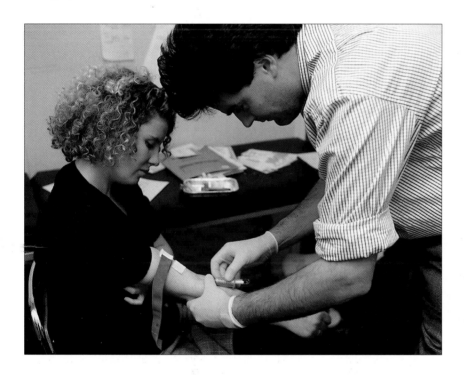

SICKLE CELL DISEASE AND THALASSAEMIA

Sickle cell disease is a blood condition that mainly affects people of African and West Indian origin, and less often, people from India, the Middle East and Mediterranean. Thalassaemia, another blood condition, mainly affects people of Mediterranean and Asian origin. If you, or your parents, come originally from these parts of the world, you'll probably be offered a blood test to find out whether you are a carrier. It is possible for either you or your partner to be a carrier without it affecting your baby at all. But if both of you are carriers, or if either of you suffer from the disease yourself, you should discuss the implications for the baby with your doctor or midwife. Or contact the Sickle Cell Society or the Thalassaemia Society (see page 127).

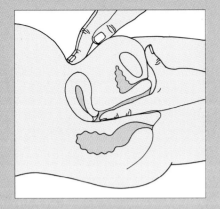

INTERNAL EXAMINATION

You may have a internal examination. By putting one or two fingers inside your vagina and pressing the other hand on your abdomen, your doctor can feel the size of your womb and judge the age of your baby. Some doctors prefer to use an ultrasound scan (see below) either at the first or a later visit.

CERVICAL SMEAR

You may be given a cervical smear test now if you haven't had one in the last three years. The test detects early changes in the cervix (neck of the womb) which could later lead to cancer. By sliding an instrument called a speculum into your vagina, the doctor can look at your cervix. A smear is then taken from the surface of the cervix which will be examined under a microscope. The test may feel a bit uncomfortable but is not painful, and won't harm the growing baby.

HERPES

If you, or your partner, have ever had genital herpes, or you get your first attack of genital blisters or ulcers during your pregnancy, let your doctor or midwife know. This is important because herpes can be dangerous for your newborn baby and he or she may need special monitoring and possibly treatment.

LATER VISITS

Later visits are usually shorter. Your weight, urine and blood pressure will be checked. Your abdomen will be felt to check the baby's position and growth. And the doctor or midwife will listen to your baby's heartbeat. Soon you will be able to listen to the heart yourself. You can also ask questions or talk about anything that is worrying you. Talking is as much a part of antenatal care as all the tests and examinations.

At first, your antenatal visits will probably be once a month. In the last two or three months of pregnancy, you'll be asked to go more often. If you can't keep an antenatal appointment, let the clinic, GP or midwife know, and make another appointment.

ULTRASOUND SCAN

This test uses sound waves to build up a picture of the baby in the womb. Most hospitals will offer women at least one ultrasound scan during their pregnancy. *An ultrasound scan can be used to:*

- check the baby's measurements. This gives quite an accurate idea of the baby's age and can help decide when your baby is likely to be born. This can be useful if you are unsure about the date of your last period
- check whether you are carrying more than one baby.

- detect some abnormalities, particularly in the baby's head or spine.
- show the position of the baby and the placenta. In some cases, for example where the placenta is low, special care may be needed in delivery.
- check that the baby is growing and developing normally.

The scan is safe and completely painless and can be carried out at any stage of pregnancy. Most hospitals scan all women at 18–20 weeks to check for certain abnormalities.

You will probably be asked to drink a lot of fluid before you have the scan. A full bladder pushes your womb up and this gives a better picture. You then lie on your back and some jelly is put on your abdomen. An instrument is passed backwards and forwards over your skin and high frequency sound is beamed through your abdomen into the womb. The sound is reflected back and creates a picture which is shown on a TV screen. It can be very exciting to see a picture of your own baby before birth – often moving about inside.

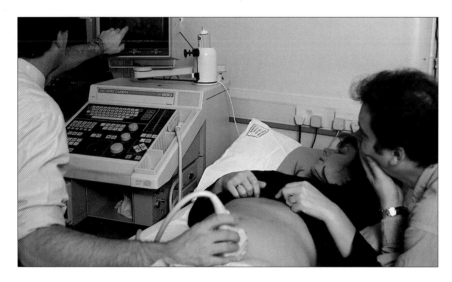

Ask for the picture to be explained to you if you can't make it out. It may be possible for your partner to come with you and see the scan. Many couples feel that this helps to make the baby real for them both. Ask if it's possible to have a copy of the picture.

If you feel doubtful about having a scan, talk it over with your GP, midwife or the hospital doctor in charge of your pregnancy.

TESTS TO DETECT ABNORMALITIES IN THE BABY

Talk to the antenatal clinic sister or doctor about these tests as they are not available in all hospitals.

ALPHA-FETOPROTEIN (AFP) TEST

This test may be performed at about 16 to 18 weeks to find out the level of alpha-fetoprotein, a protein from the baby, in your blood. Small amounts of this protein are made by the baby and pass into

Tests to detect abnormalities in the baby

Before making up your mind, about these tests talk to your doctor or midwife and find out all you want to know. You may also want to talk it over with your partner or a friend. If the test shows that your baby is likely to be born with a serious disability, you should be offered the choice of whether or not to continue with the pregnancy. It may be better for you to discuss this before the test. You do not have to make up your mind in advance and even if you do not want a termination you may still want the test. It can either reassure you that your baby is likely to be born healthy or will give you time to prepare for having a baby with special needs.

your blood during pregnancy. If the level is higher or lower than normal there is a chance that your baby may be at risk from either spina bifida or Down's syndrome. However it is still only a chance. Another blood test may be given as a double check and further screening such as ultrasound or amniocentesis will give you more definite information.

Some hospitals routinely test for alpha-fetoprotein. Others don't. If you want the test and it is not offered, ask for it well in advance.

'TRIPLE' OR 'TRIPLE PLUS' TEST

This is a new blood test for Down's syndrome. It combines the AFP result with the levels of other blood chemicals to suggest how likely an abnormality might be. It's still being tested and is only available in some areas. There is usually a charge for this test. Talk to your doctor about having this test.

ULTRASOUND

Ultrasound can be used to detect Down's syndrome if it is done before 12 weeks of pregnancy. You should enquire about this possibility at your hospital as it may save you having an amniocentesis.

AMNIOCENTESIS

This test may be offered at about 12 to 18 weeks of pregnancy:

- to older women for whom there is a higher risk of having a baby with Down's syndrome.
- when a woman's family history suggests that there may be a risk of her baby having Down's syndrome, spina bifida, muscular dystrophy, haemophilia or cystic fibrosis.
- when the blood test for alpha-fetoprotein or triple test shows that the baby may be at risk of Down's syndrome or spina bifida. In the case of spina bifida a detailed ultrasound scan may provide enough information.

An ultrasound scan will always be done first to check the position of the baby and the placenta. Then, after a local anaesthetic, a needle is passed through the wall of the abdomen into the amniotic fluid which surrounds the baby. A sample of the fluid is drawn off and sent to the laboratory for testing.

Results for spina bifida are known in a few days. The Down's syndrome test is more complex and results take longer. This same test will also reveal the baby's sex. Tell your doctor whether or not you want to know what it is. If there is haemophilia or muscular dystrophy in your family, it is important to know your baby's sex. If you are carrying a boy, he may inherit the disease.

Although every care will be taken in carrying out an amniocentesis, the test does involve a small risk. Less than one in 100 tests results in a miscarriage. In deciding whether or not to go ahead with the test, you need to balance this risk against the value of the test to you. For example, you may feel a very strong need to know whether your baby has any disability. You should remember that a normal test does not absolutely guarantee that there will be no problems, but it is reassuring.

CHORIONIC VILLUS SAMPLING (CVS)

This new test, at present only available in a few large hospitals and clinics, can show up a number of disorders in the developing baby. The advantage is that it can be carried out early in pregnancy, between 8 to 11 weeks. However, the risk of causing a miscarriage is somewhat higher than for amniocentesis. *This test may be offered to:*

- older women who are at higher risk of having a baby with Down's syndrome.
- women at risk of having a child with certain inherited diseases, such as sickle cell anaemia or thalassaemia.

It will not show spina bifida.

The test, which is not painful, takes between 10 and 20 minutes. Using ultrasound as a guide, a fine tube is passed through the vagina and cervix, or sometimes through the abdomen, and a small piece of the developing placenta, known as chorionic tissue, is withdrawn. The results take one to two weeks, often less.

If you feel the test would be helpful, talk over the matter carefully with your GP or midwife early in pregnancy, as well as with your partner or a close friend. You can also contact your regional genetics centre direct (telephone the Genetics Interest Group - see page 126 - for the address and telephone number of your nearest centre).

MAKING THE MOST OF ANTENATAL CARE

Attending regularly for antenatal care is important for your health and the health of your baby. However, sometimes antenatal visits can seem quite an effort. If the clinic is busy or short-staffed you may have to wait a long time, and if you have small children with you, this can be very exhausting. Try to plan ahead to make your visits easier and come prepared to wait. *Here are some suggestions:*

- In some clinics you can buy refreshments. If not, take a snack with you if you are likely to get hungry.
- Write a list of any questions you want to ask and take it with you to remind you. Make sure you get answers to your questions or the opportunity to discuss any worries. Sometimes this can take quite a lot of determination.
- If your partner is free he may be able to go with you. He'll be able to support you in discussing any worries or in finding out what you want to know. It will also help him to feel more involved in your pregnancy.

"I think it's up to you to make the most of it. You can find out a lot, but you have to ask. When your blood pressure's taken, you have to say 'Is that alright?' Then they'll tell you. And if it's not alright, you have to ask why not, and talk about it. It's the same for everything. It's not being a nuisance, it's being interested. I think the staff like it if you're interested."

"There were some things that really annoyed me - the gowns, and the lavatories, and one midwife who called everyone 'sweetie'. But there were other things I wouldn't have missed - like hearing my baby's heart beating, and well, just knowing she was alright. Knowing I was alright too, come to that."

YOUR ANTENATAL NOTES

At your first antenatal visit, your doctor or midwife will enter your details in a record book and add to them at each visit. Many hospitals ask women to look after these notes themselves. Other hospitals keep the notes and give you a card which records your details.

This is just a sample of the information your card or notes may contain, as each clinic has its own. Always ask your doctor or midwife about anything on your card which you would like to have explained.

Take your notes or card with you wherever you go. Then if you need medical attention while you are away from home, you will have with you the information that's needed.

Urine These are the results of your urine tests for protein and sugar. '+' or 'Tr' means a quantity (or trace) has been found. 'Alb' stand for 'albumin', - a name for one of the proteins detected in urine. 'Nil', or a tick, or 'NAD' all mean the same: 'nothing abnormal discovered'. 'Ketones' may be found if you have not eaten recently or have been vomiting.

Blood pressure (BP) This usually stays at about the same level throughout pregnancy. If it goes up a lot in the last half of pregnancy, it can be dangerous for your baby.

Fetal heart 'FHH', or just 'H' means 'fetal heart heard'. 'FMF' means 'fetal movement felt'.

Oedema This is another word for swelling, most often of the feet and hands. Usually it is nothing to worry about but tell your doctor or midwife if it suddenly gets worse.

Hb stands for 'haemoglobin'. This is tested in your blood sample to check you are not anaemic.

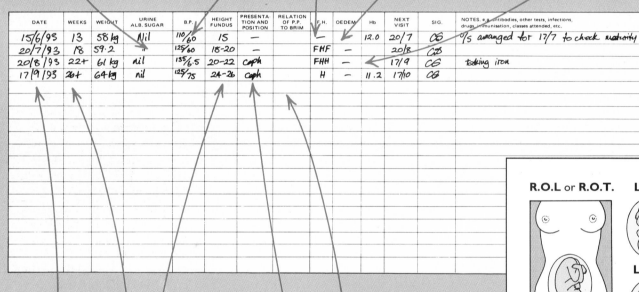

DATE	WEEKS	WEIGHT	URINE ALB. SUGAR	B.P.	HEIGHT FUNDUS	PRESENTA-TION AND POSITION	RELATION OF P.P. TO BRIM	F.H.	OEDEM	Hb	NEXT VISIT	SIG.	NOTES. e.g. antibodies, other tests, infections, drugs, immunisation, classes attended, etc.
15/6/93	13	58 kg	Nil	110/60	15	—		—		12.0	20/7	OG	U/s arranged for 12/7 to check maturity
20/7/93	18	59.2	"	125/60	18-20	—		FMF	—		20/8	CB	
20/8/93	22+	61 kg	nil	135/6.5	20-22	Ceph		FHH	—		17/9	CG	taking iron
17/9/93	26+	64 kg	nil	125/75	24-26	Ceph		H	—	11.2	17/10	CG	

Date The date of your antenatal visit.

Weeks The length of your pregnancy in weeks from the date of your last monthly period.

Height of fundus By gently pressing on your abdomen, the doctor can feel your womb. Early in pregnancy the top of the womb, or the 'fundus', can be felt low down, below your navel. Towards the end, it is well up above your navel, just under your breasts. So the height of the fundus is a guide to how many weeks pregnant you are.

This column gives the length of your pregnancy, in weeks, estimated according to the position of the fundus. The figure should be roughly the

Height of Fundus

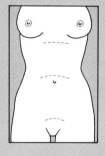

same as the figure in the 'weeks' column. If there's a big difference, (say, more than two weeks) ask your doctor about it. Sometimes the height of the fundus may be measured with a tape measure and the result entered on your card in centimetres.

Relation to brim. This is where your baby's head is in relation to the brim of your pelvis. It may be described in how many fifths of the head can be felt above the brim.

'E' or 'eng' means 'engaged'. That is, the baby's head has moved down into the pelvis ready for birth. This may happen a few weeks before the birth, or not until you are in labour. 'NE' means 'not engaged'.

Presentation is which way up the baby is. Up to about 30 weeks, the baby moves about a lot. Then it usually settles into its head downwards position, ready to be born head first. This is recorded as 'Vx' (vertex) or 'C' or 'ceph' (cephalic). Both words mean the top of the head. If your

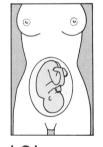

R.O.L or R.O.T.   **L.O.P.**

L.O.A.

L.O.L. or L.O.T.   **R.O.A.**   **R.O.P.**

Position Abbreviations are used to describe the way the baby is lying - facing sideways, for example, or frontwards or backwards. Ask your midwife to explain the way your baby is lying.

baby stays with its bottom downwards, this is a 'breech' (Br) presentation. 'PP' means presenting part - the bit of the baby that is coming first.

WHO'S WHO?

During your pregnancy and after your baby's birth, you will meet a lot of people who will be involved in your care. It can be quite confusing! Professionals should, of course, introduce themselves and explain what they do, but if they forget, don't hesitate to ask. It may help to make a note of who you have seen and what they have said in case you need to discuss any point later on.

These are the people you're most likely to meet. Some may have students with them who are training.

- **Midwives** are specially trained to care for mothers and babies throughout normal pregnancy, labour and after the birth. They either work in hospital or in the community. Some may rotate between the two.
- A **hospital midwife** or **doctor** will probably see you each time you go to a hospital antenatal clinic. A midwife will look after you during labour and will probably deliver your baby, if your delivery is normal. You and your baby will be looked after by midwives and nurses on the postnatal ward until you go home. You will probably also meet student midwives.
- A **community midwife** will probably get to know you before your baby is born and will visit you at home, after you leave hospital, during the early weeks. Community midwives are sometimes attached to GPs' practices and may be involved in giving antenatal care. They are also involved in delivering babies at community and GP / midwife units and are responsible for home deliveries. Some community midwives also accompany women into the hospital maternity unit to be with them for the birth.
- Your **general practitioner (GP)** will help you to plan your antenatal care. This may be given at the hospital, but it is quite often shared with the GP.

Sometimes the GP may be responsible for all your antenatal care. If you have your baby in a community or GP/midwife unit, your GP may be involved in your baby's delivery. If your baby is born in hospital, your GP will be notified of your baby's birth and will arrange to see you soon after you return home. Don't forget to register your baby with your GP.

- An **obstetrician**, is a doctor specialising in the care of women during pregnancy, labour and soon after the birth. If you are having a hospital birth you will be under the care of a consultant and the doctors on his or her own team together with other professionals, such as midwives. If everything is straightforward, a midwife will usually deliver your baby. You may only see your obstetrician once or twice during your pregnancy, with most of your care provided by midwives, shared with your doctor, but this depends on local arrangements. You should ask for an appointment with your consultant if you wish to discuss any matter you think is important.

- A **paediatrician** is a doctor specialising in the care of babies and children. The paediatrician may check your baby after the birth to make sure all is well. If your baby should have any problems, you will be able to talk this over with the paediatrician.
- A **physiotherapist** is specially trained to help you cope with the physical changes of pregnancy, childbirth and afterwards. You may meet her during antenatal classes and after your baby is born. She'll show you the best exercises to help your muscles recover.
- **Health visitors** are nurses with extra training in caring for people in the community. They are concerned with the health of the whole family. The health visitor will visit you at home some time after your baby is ten days old to offer support and help with any worries or problems. You may continue to see your health visitor, either at home, or at your child health clinic, health centre or GP's surgery, depending on where she is based.

"Being shown the delivery suite helped us - just knowing what to expect made it less scary."

"It really helped me to make up my mind about how I wanted to have my baby."

"It was great meeting people who were going through the same things I was."

"It was brilliant having classes in the evening because it meant Phil could help me during labour."

ANTENATAL CLASSES

Antenatal classes can help to prepare you for your baby's birth and for looking after your baby. They can also help you to keep yourself fit and well during pregnancy. They are sometimes called parentcraft or 'preparation for parenthood' or 'ready for baby' groups. They're a good chance to meet other parents, to talk about things that might be worrying you and to ask questions - and make new friends. They are usually informal and fun.

You may be able to go to some introductory classes on babycare early in pregnancy. Otherwise, many classes will start about eight to ten weeks before your baby is due.

Classes are normally held once a week, either during the day or in the evening, and last one or two hours. Some classes are for women only. Others will welcome partners, either to all the sessions or to some of them, or you can go alone or with a friend.

In some areas there are classes especially for women whose first language is not English. *The kind of topics covered by antenatal classes are:*

- health in pregnancy
- what happens during labour and birth
- coping with labour and information about pain relief
- exercises to keep you fit during pregnancy and help you in labour
- relaxation
- caring for your baby, including feeding
- your own health after the birth

Think about what you hope to gain from antenatal classes, so that if there is a choice you can find the sort of class that suits you best. You need to start making inquiries early in pregnancy so that you can be sure of getting a place in the class you choose. You can go to more than one class. Ask your hospital midwife, your community midwife or health visitor or your GP, or the local branch of the National Childbirth Trust (see page 125).

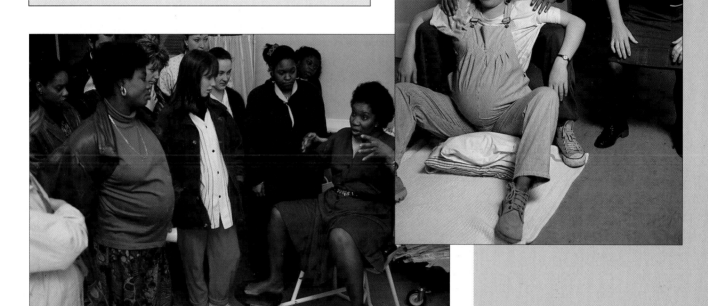

Some classes will try to cover all these topics. Others will concentrate more on certain aspects, such as exercises and relaxation or babycare.

The number of different antenatal classes available varies very much from place to place. Classes may be run by your hospital, by your local midwives or health visitors, by your own GP or health centre.

Antenatal classes may give you the opportunity to get to know some of the professionals involved in your care, and to ask questions and talk over any worries you may have. You can find out about arrangements for labour and birth and the sort of choices available to you. This can help you in thinking about making your own birth plan (see page 32). You'll usually be able to look round the labour and postnatal wards. You may also be able to meet some of the people who will be looking after you when the time comes for your baby to be born.

Classes can give you confidence as well as information. You'll be able to talk over any worries and discuss your plans, not just with professionals, but with other parents as well.

Speak to your community midwife if you can't go to classes. She may have videos to lend you or you may be able to rent or buy one.

8 The feeding question

"It was so easy. I suppose it took me about a couple of weeks to get used to it, and from then on I just didn't have to think. It was the one thing that wasn't any effort at all."

"Breastfeeding was so difficult what with one thing and another - first the baby was ill, then me. I'd be crying. The baby would be crying and hungry. So we started on the bottle and somehow from then on it was alright and I felt much better about it all".

"I didn't want to breastfeed. It was as simple as that. The whole idea of it put me off and I just couldn't have done it".

"I had quite a few problems at first with sore nipples and one thing and another. It made it difficult. I think I'd have given up if it hadn't been for the midwife. She was ever so good. And after a while it all sorted out and now I'm glad I did it".

It's never too early to start thinking about how you're going to feed your baby. Once your baby is born there will be lots to occupy you ! You'll need to discuss it with other people, the baby's father, your midwife, health visitor or other mothers.

Breastfeeding is best for the health of your baby but it's just as important that you feel happy and comfortable about the choice you have made. You can't know in advance what breastfeeding will be like but you can always decide to breastfeed at first and then change to bottle feeding if it really doesn't work out. It's more difficult to change from bottle to breastfeeding. If you don't breastfeed at all you may later regret that you never had the experience.

Some mothers have definite reasons for choosing to bottle feed. The best way to feed your baby is the way that feels right for you.

If you're HIV positive you will be advised not to breast feed because of the small risk of passing the virus on to your baby through the milk. It is a good idea to discuss this with your doctor, midwife or health visitor.

BREASTFEEDING

WHY BREAST IS BEST FOR BABIES

- Breast milk gives your baby exactly the right food. It contains everything a baby needs.
- Breast milk is easily digested and unlikely to cause stomach upsets.
- Breast milk contains antibodies which help protect your baby from coughs, colds, chest and stomach infections. Powdered milk does not contain these antibodies.
- Breastfed babies are very unlikely to become constipated as the milk is right for the baby. Stools are usually soft and easy to pass out, as well as less smelly than those of bottle fed babies.
- Breastfed babies are less likely to develop allergies.
- Breastfed babies are less likely to get fat. They take just as much milk as they need - they don't need any extra fluids. There is always some breast milk available at the right temperature for a hungry or thirsty baby.
- Breast milk adapts itself to your baby's changing needs as you feed.
- If your baby is born prematurely there will be definite health benefits if you breastfeed.

WHY BREAST IS BEST FOR MOTHERS

As this mother said: *"It was feeling close, and being together, that was what I liked"* but there are other benefits too:

- Breastfeeding costs nothing.
- There's no need to prepare feeds or wash and sterilise bottles.
- Your baby isn't kept waiting for a feed.
- Breastfeeding helps to get your shape back sooner because it uses up calories.
- It's so much easier in the middle of the night.

SOME OF YOUR QUESTIONS ANSWERED

Can all women breast feed?
Almost every woman can breast feed, but it can sometimes take a little while to get it going. Be patient and ask for help if you need it.

Does breast size matter?
No. All shapes and sizes make milk.

Can flat or inverted nipples be a problem?
Most women with flat or inverted nipples should be able to breast feed. However, you may need a little extra help in learning to position your baby (see page 61).

Do I need to prepare my breasts for breastfeeding?
Your breasts will prepare themselves naturally, although it's a good idea to try to keep your skin soft and supple - so avoid soaps and sprays that have a drying effect.

If my baby is born prematurely, will it have the energy to suck at the breast?
You can only wait and see. Small babies will benefit if they get some mother's milk.

How can I make sure my partner feels involved?
Breastfeeding is only one way to be close to a baby. Babies need cuddling, bathing and lots more attention.

Can I go out without the baby?
Yes. You can always express some of your milk and leave it for someone else to give your baby (see page 63).

Is it worth breastfeeding if I am going back to work soon?
Yes. The early weeks, while you are at home, are the time when breast milk does the most good. After that you can express your breast milk or use powdered milk for your baby while you are at work and continue to breastfeed at other times.

"I really enjoy the closeness of breastfeeding and my partner says it makes him feel so proud, watching us together."

"I wasn't sure if I'd be able to breastfeed. My mum bottle fed me so she couldn't help. Once I got going though, it was so easy. I can't think why I was so unsure at first now."

What about feeding my baby in front of friends?

You may be quite happy about feeding in front of others. If you feel uneasy, you could feed the baby discreetly under a loose top, t-shirt or half-unbuttoned blouse.

Breastfeeding a baby can be a great pleasure. Even if it doesn't go well for you at the start, it's still worth working at. Although problems with breastfeeding, even quite small problems, can be quite upsetting, they can almost always be overcome. *You can get help from:*

- your community midwife or health visitor.
- a breastfeeding counsellor or support group. Contact your local branch of the National Childbirth Trust, or the La Leche League (page 125). These organisations give help and support through other mothers who have experience of breastfeeding.

Don't worry if other mothers seem to be doing things differently. It is important to have confidence in yourself and your baby so that together you can work out what is best for both of you.

THE FIRST FEW DAYS

In the beginning, it can seem that you are doing nothing but feeding but gradually your baby will settle into a pattern of feeding. Try to relax into it and take each day as it comes.

For the first few days after birth your breasts produce a special food called **colostrum**, which looks like rich creamy milk and is sometimes quite yellow in colour. This contains all the food your baby needs, as well as antibodies which pass your own resistance to certain infections on to your baby.

After about three days your breasts will begin to produce milk which will look quite thin compared with colostrum. Different kinds of milk are now produced each time you feed your baby. The **fore milk**, which your baby takes first, is thirst quenching and means your baby gets a drink at the start of every feed. A breastfed baby doesn't need any other drinks (including infant teas or juices), even in hot weather, as long as you feed whenever the baby asks. The fore milk is then followed by the richer **hind milk**, which is the food part of the feed and contains the calories your baby needs.

Your breasts may become very large and heavy for a while and may feel uncomfortable, or even painful, at first.

Milk may leak from your nipples and you may feel more comfortable wearing breast pads. Change them frequently. Avoid plastic backs. Or you can use clean cotton hankies, and at night you could put a clean towel under you instead of wearing pads.

Gradually the amount of milk you produce will settle down and your breasts will begin to feel normal again. If you are very uncomfortable, ask your midwife for help.

Relaxation

You need to be fairly relaxed to breastfeed. Stress, worry, exhaustion, pain, even embarrassment, can all stop the 'let-down' reflex working. You stand a much better chance of breastfeeding successfully if you can relax and care for yourself.

Nursing bras

A nursing bra will give you support so that you feel more comfortable. Choose adjustable bras because the size of your breasts will change (see page 78). Some women feel more comfortable wearing a nursing bra at night as well.

HOW TO BREASTFEED

This is a new skill, so you should ask your midwife to show you how. These hints will give you a few basic ideas.

First find a comfortable position, either sitting upright, well-supported or lying down.

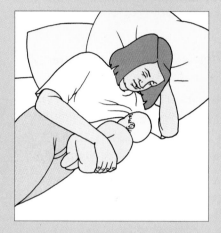

Then turn your baby towards you with the head opposite your breast, and the nose lined up with your nipple. Support your baby with a hand across the shoulders not behind the head.

Now brush your baby's lips against your nipple to get her to open her mouth really wide, then draw your baby to your breast quickly. If your baby is correctly positioned, there will be more of your areola showing above the top lip than below the bottom lip.

Start each feed on alternate sides. Let your baby decide when he or she has finished the first breast before switching to the second. Sometimes babies only need one breast at a feed.

Many babies develop a pattern of feeding, but you need not let the baby wait for a feed, nor restrict the length of the feed.

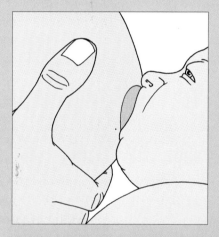

Important points to remember

● If your baby just feeds on the nipple, he or she will get very little milk and you may become sore.

● If feeding feels wrong or hurts or your baby doesn't seem to be feeding properly, stop the feed. Break the suction by putting your little finger into the corner of your baby's mouth. Adjust the position and start again.

What you eat and drink
Breastfeeding uses up energy and fluid and you will probably be hungrier and thirstier than usual. Eat and drink when you feel you need to. It will help to keep you going and keep up your milk supply. Remember whatever you eat and drink passes into your breast milk. It's a good idea not to drink too much alcohol. About one or two units, once or twice a week is the best advice during pregnancy. And too much coffee or cola may upset you and your baby. You should always ask your doctor, dentist or pharmacist before taking any medicine or remedy, whether it is prescribed or bought over the counter. If you smoke, some of the nicotine will pass into your baby's bloodstream (see page 10).

HOW BREASTFEEDING WORKS

Your milk supply Your breasts produce milk in answer to your baby feeding at your breast. The more your baby feeds, the more your body makes milk, provided that your baby is correctly positioned. If you reduce feeding, you will make less milk.

The let-down reflex Your baby's sucking causes milk to gather behind the nipple, ready for feeding. This is called the 'let-down' reflex. You will see quick sucks change to deep swallows once the milk has begun to flow. Babies pause while they wait for more milk to be 'delivered'. It is not normal for a baby to suck non stop!

HOW OFTEN AND HOW MUCH

It's best to feed when your baby wants to be fed. This might be very often at first, though feeds will become more spaced out as your baby gets older. Some babies settle into their own pattern quite quickly. Others take longer.

From time to time, your baby will have a growth spurt - the first may occur around ten days old. When this happens, your baby needs more milk and you may find that feeds are longer and more frequent for a while. Don't panic and feel you need to offer extra bottles of powdered milk. You'll be able to make more milk in response to your baby's demands.

The sucking process releases milk to satisfy your baby, and stimulates the production of more. When your baby is full up, he or she will stop feeding. A good sign that your baby is getting enough milk is at least six wet nappies every 24 hours without any other drinks. If you're worried, your midwife or health visitor will be able to check the weight of your baby and make sure all is well.

HOW TO OVERCOME COMMON DIFFICULTIES

The quicker you sort out any difficulties in breastfeeding, the better for you and your baby. So don't hesitate to ask for help immediately. Many women are surprised to find that most problems are quite easily overcome by a slight change to their baby's position when feeding, or by feeding their baby more often.

Feeding restlessly If your baby is restless at the breast and doesn't seem satisfied by feeds, it may be that he or she is sucking on the nipple alone and so not getting enough milk. Ask for help in making sure your baby feeds in the right position.

Engorged breasts A few days after the birth, your breasts may become very swollen (engorged) and uncomfortable. The answer is to breastfeed. If feeding is difficult for any reason, ask your midwife for help, or make sure you have the telephone number of a breastfeeding counsellor. A good supporting bra will help too, but make sure it isn't too tight.

Sore or cracked nipples If your nipples are sore when you're feeding, your baby's position will need adjusting. *The following suggestions may also help:*

- keep your nipples dry and expose them to the air as much as you can. Try sleeping topless if it's warm enough, with a towel under you if you're leaking milk.
- change your breast pads frequently (use pads without plastic).
- avoid soap as it dries the skin.
- wear a cotton bra which allows air to circulate.
- try squeezing out a drop or two of your milk at the end of a feed and gently rubbing it into your skin.

If you suddenly get sore and pink nipples after any first soreness has passed, you might have an infection known as thrush. Go and see your GP.

Lumpy tender breasts These are often caused by blocked milk ducts, and there are a number of things you can do to help:

- let your baby feed on the tender breast first or, if he or she doesn't want to feed, try expressing some milk.
- while your baby is feeding, gently stroke the lumpy area with your fingertips, smoothing the milk towards your nipple.
- try leaning over your baby as you feed.

It's important to deal with a blocked duct as soon as possible to make sure that it doesn't lead to mastitis.

Mastitis If you have mastitis your breasts will feel hot and tender and you may feel as though you have flu. If this occurs, continue to breastfeed but get a midwife or health visitor to check your position. See your GP if there is no improvement within six to eight hours.

WIND

Babies always take in air as they feed, some more than others. After a feed, gentle back rubbing with your baby lying against your shoulder or held a little forward on your lap may bring up some wind that would be uncomfortable otherwise. Don't worry if you don't get any up. It is not essential. It may even be that there is none to come. Sometimes a little milk is brought up at the same time. This is known as 'posset' - and it's normal.

EXPRESSING MILK

You may wish to express your breast milk and leave it in a bottle for someone else to give your baby if, for example, you want to go out for the evening. Your midwife or health visitor will show you how to do it. You can do it by hand or use a breast pump.

There are different types of breast pump, so ask advice on which to choose. If you use a pump, make sure you sterilise it before and after use.

Store the expressed milk in a sterilised bottle with the top screwed on in the fridge. Never keep for longer than 24 hours. You can also deep freeze expressed milk but ask for advice on how to store and defrost safely first.

BOTTLE FEEDING

Bottle feeding may seem like hard work at first until you get into a routine of sterilising bottles and preparing feeds. Once you're organised, you'll be able to relax and really enjoy feeding. Feeding is the best time to hold your baby close in your arms and one advantage of bottle feeding is that fathers can share in this enjoyment.

a father: *"Because Ellen was bottle fed we both fed her. I used to do it in the evenings and most of the feeds at weekends. We started to do it to give Karen a rest, but in the end I wanted to do it. It brought the baby closer. She's very close to me now."*

Feeding is a time for getting to know your baby and feeling close. But remember, even when your baby is a little older, he or she should never be left alone to feed with a propped up bottle, in case of choking.

BABY MILK (INFANT FORMULA)

Baby milk, also called infant formula or artificial milk, usually comes in powder form. It is usually cow's milk that has been specially treated so that babies can digest it. And it has the right balance of vitamins and minerals for a young baby. Baby milks based on soya protein are also available but they are not usually given at this young age.

Ordinary cow's milk, condensed milk, evaporated milk, dried milk, goat's milk, or any other type of milk should never be given to a baby. They are not suitable. If you have any worries about the baby milk you are giving your baby, ask advice from your midwife, health visitor or GP.

There are a number of different brands of baby milk available in the shops. 'Ready-to-feed' baby milks in cartons are also available in some places. This is generally more expensive than powdered

milk, but may be useful in an emergency or if you're away from home. Once opened, the carton should be stored in the fridge and thrown away after 24 hours.

Although formula milk contains vitamins, you may be advised to give your baby vitamin drops from the age of one month onwards. You can buy these at the child health clinic.

BOTTLES AND TEATS

You'll need at least six bottles and teats. This is to make sure that you always have at least one or two bottles clean, sterilised and ready for use. Ask your midwife, health visitor or other mothers if you want advice on what kind to buy.

You should always buy new teats and it's best if you can buy new bottles too. Check regularly to make sure the bottles are in good condition. If they're badly scratched, you won't be able to sterilise them properly. If in doubt, ask your midwife or health visitor for advice.

MAKING UP THE FEED

When you're preparing formula milk, always follow the instructions on the tin exactly. The milk powder has been very carefully balanced for your baby. So don't be tempted to add extra powder to make a 'stronger feed' as this could be harmful to your baby. And don't add any sugar, honey or anything else.

If you're worried, your midwife or health visitor will advise you how much milk your baby is likely to need. If you make up more than your baby wants, throw away what is left at the end of the feed. You will probably find it suits your routine to make up a number of feeds in advance. Cool the capped bottles quickly under cold running water, and put them in the fridge as soon as possible. Don't keep the made up milk for longer than 24 hours.

> **If you're on Income Support, you can get tokens for free milk and vitamins for your baby or a free pint of milk for you if you're breastfeeding (see page 122).**

> **Using bottled water**
> **If you use bottled water to make up a feed, for example, on holiday, it must be boiled first. It's better to use spring water rather than mineral water. Use flat water, not fizzy.**

Preparing a feed

1. Make sure your hands are absolutely clean.

2. Boil some water in the kettle and let it cool.

3. Take a sterilised bottle and teat.

4. Take the cooled water and fill the bottle to the right place using the measuring marks.

5. Measure the exact amount of powder using the special scoop provided with the milk. Level off the powder in the scoop using a clean dry knife. Don't pack the powder down at all.

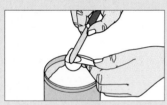

6. Add the powder to the water in the bottle.

7. Screw on the cap and shake well until the powder has dissolved.

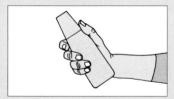

8. Store the bottle in the fridge if you're not using it straight away.

FEEDING

Your baby will gradually settle into a routine. Babies vary in how often they want to feed and how much they want to take. Some may be content with feeds every three to four hours and others may want smaller quantities more often. Respond to your baby's needs and feed when he or she is hungry, just as you would if you were breastfeeding. In the same way, don't try to force your baby to finish a bottle. He or she may have had enough for the time being or simply want a rest.

- **The temperature of the milk** Before you start to feed your baby always check that the milk is not too hot by dripping some on the inside of your wrist. Some babies don't mind cold milk. Others prefer it warm. If you want to warm the milk a little, place the bottle upright in some hot water, keeping the teat out of the water. Don't keep the milk warm for more than 20 minutes before the feed, as germs can breed in the warmth. Never warm the milk in a microwave oven as this is unsafe. The milk continues to heat for a time after you take it out of the microwave, although the outside of the bottle may feel cold. The milk inside may be very hot and could scald your baby's mouth.
- **Have everything you need ready before you start feeding.**
- **A comfortable position** Find a comfortable position in which you can hold your baby while you are feeding. Give your baby time. Some babies take some milk, pause for a nap and then wake up for more. So be patient.
- **The teat** As you feed, keep the bottle tilted so that the teat is always full of milk. Otherwise your baby will be taking in air. If the teat becomes flattened while you are feeding pull gently on the bottle to release the vacuum. If the teat becomes blocked, replace it with another sterile teat. Teats do come in different shapes and with different hole sizes. You may have to try several before you find the one that suits your baby. If the hole is too small your baby will not get enough milk. If it's too big it will come too fast. Check that the teat is not torn or damaged.
- **After the feed** Gently rub or pat your baby's back for a while to see whether there is any wind to come up. There's no need to overdo this. Wind is not such a problem as many people think. But your baby will probably enjoy the rubbing and closeness to you after the feed.
- **Don't forget to throw away unused milk in the bottle.**
- **Water** If your baby cries between feeds, it may be because of thirst rather than hunger. Try giving a bottle of cooled, boiled water. Don't forget that the bottle must be sterilised too. It can help to give your baby boiled, cooled water if he or she is constipated. There's no need to give your baby any other drinks besides milk or water.

Your midwife or health visitor will chat to you about feeding when they call. Talk to them about any worries or problems.

CLEANING AND STERILISING

It's important to keep bottles and teats, and other equipment used in feeding, absolutely clean to protect your baby against infection. This means sterilising as well as washing. There are a number of different ways to do this. *You can use:*

- **A chemical steriliser.** There are several different brands in the shops. They consist of a sterilising tank to which you add cold water and a sterilising tablet or liquid.
- **A steam steriliser.** This is a very quick and efficient method of sterilising.
- **A microwave bottle steriliser.** Without this equipment, a microwave alone is not enough to sterilise the bottles.

Ask your midwife, health visitor or other mothers about the different methods and which might be most appropriate for you. If you buy equipment, make sure you follow the manufacturer's instructions.

Chemical sterilisation

1. Wash the bottles, teats and other equipment thoroughly in hot water using washing up liquid. Get rid of every trace of milk using a bottle brush for the inside of the bottles. You may have been advised to use salt to clean the teats. Use as little as possible and make sure that it's rinsed off thoroughly. Squirt water through the teats. This will make sure the holes are clear.

2. Rinse thoroughly in clean running water.

3. To make up the solution, follow the instructions that come with the sterilising tablets or liquid. Put the bottles and teats and other equipment (but nothing metal) in the solution and leave for the time given in the instructions. The tank will have a floating lid that keeps everything under the water or you can use a large plate to keep the bottles immersed. Make sure there are no air bubbles inside the bottles. Put the teats and caps in upside down to prevent air being trapped. Once the equipment is sterilised you should not add new items or the whole solution will be contaminated.

4. Make sure your hands are absolutely clean when you take out the bottles and teats to make up the feeds. If you want to rinse off the sterilising solution, use cooled boiled water. Do not use tap water as this will make them unsterile again.

9 Problems

COMMON MINOR PROBLEMS

Your body has a great deal to do during pregnancy. Sometimes the changes taking place will cause irritation, discomfort or, on occasions, may seem quite alarming. There is rarely any need for alarm but you should mention anything that is worrying you at your next appointment with your doctor or midwife.

If you think that something may be seriously wrong, trust your own judgement, and get in touch with your doctor or midwife straightaway.

We have listed, in alphabetical order, the changes you are most likely to notice and their causes - where these are known - and suggestions on how to cope.

BACKACHE

During pregnancy some body tissues become softer to prepare you for labour. This can put a strain on the muscles and joints of the lower back. The extra weight you are carrying can also cause strain. As you get larger you may start to tip backwards to balance the weight in front. This can cause backache or make it worse.

To avoid backache:

- avoid heavy lifting.
- bend your knees and keep your back straight when lifting or picking something up from the floor.
- if you do have to carry something heavy, hold it close to your body.
- move your feet when turning round to avoid twisting your spine
- wear flat shoes as these allow your weight to be evenly distributed
- work at a surface high enough to prevent you stooping.
- try to balance the weight between two baskets if you are carrying shopping.
- sit with your back straight and well supported.

A firm mattress can help to prevent and relieve backache. If your mattress is too soft, a piece of hardboard under the length will make it firmer.

Massage can also help. And make sure you get enough rest, particularly later in pregnancy.

If your backache is very painful, ask your doctor to refer you to an obstetric physiotherapist at your hospital. He or she will be able to give you some advice and suggest some helpful exercises.

CONSTIPATION

You may become constipated very early in pregnancy because of the hormonal changes going on in your body. *It will help to:*

- make sure you include plenty of fibre in your diet through eating foods like wholemeal bread, wholegrain cereals, fruit and vegetables and pulses such as beans and lentils.
- exercise regularly to keep your muscles toned up.
- make sure you drink plenty of water.
- avoid iron pills if they cause constipation. Ask your doctor whether you can manage without them or change to a different type. If not, you may have to accept having constipation.

CRAMP

Cramp is a sudden, sharp pain in your legs or feet. It usually happens at night but nobody really knows what causes it. It usually helps if you pull your toes hard up towards your ankle or rub the muscle hard.

Regular, gentle exercise in pregnancy, particularly ankle and leg movements will improve your circulation and may help to prevent cramp from occurring.

FAINTNESS

Pregnant women often feel faint. This happens when not enough blood is getting to the brain. If the oxygen level gets too low you may actually faint. It's more common in pregnancy because of hormonal changes taking place in your body. You're most likely to feel faint if you stand still for too long or get up too quickly from a chair. It often happens when you are lying on your back.

- Try to get up slowly after sitting or lying down.
- If you feel faint when standing still, find a seat quickly and the faintness will pass. If it doesn't, lie down on your side.
- If you feel faint while lying on your back, turn on to your side. It's better not to lie on your back in later pregnancy.

FEELING HOT IN PREGNANCY

During pregnancy you're likely to feel warmer than normal. This is due to hormonal changes and to an increase in blood supply to the skin. You're also likely to sweat more. *It helps if you:*

- wear loose clothing made of natural fibres, as these are more absorbent and 'breathe' more than synthetic fibres
- keep your room cool
- wash frequently to stay fresh.

HEADACHES

Some pregnant women find they get a lot of headaches. A brisk walk may be all you need, as well as a little more regular rest and relaxation. Although it is wise to avoid drugs in pregnancy, an occasional paracetamol tablet is generally considered safe.

If you often have bad headaches, tell your doctor or midwife so that they can advise you. Severe headaches may be a sign of high blood pressure (see page 75).

INDIGESTION AND HEARTBURN

This may be partly caused by the growing womb pressing on the stomach. *If you suffer from indigestion :*

- try eating smaller meals more often.
- sit up straight when you are eating. This takes the pressure off your stomach.
- avoid particular foods, for example highly spiced ones, which cause trouble but make sure you are still eating well. (See page 8 for information on healthy eating.)

Heartburn is more than just indigestion. It is a strong, burning pain in the chest. It is caused by the valve between your stomach and the tube leading to your stomach, relaxing in pregnancy, so that stomach acid passes into the tube. It is often brought on by lying flat. *To avoid heartburn you could:*

- sleep well propped up. Try raising the head of your bed with bricks or have plenty of pillows.
- try drinking a glass of milk. Have one by your bed in case you wake with heartburn in the night.
- avoiding eating or drinking for a few hours before you go to bed.
- ask your doctor's advice.

ITCHING

Mild itching is common in pregnancy because of the increased blood supply to the skin. In late pregnancy the skin of the abdomen is stretched and this may also cause itchiness. Wearing loose clothing may help.

Itching can, however, be a sign of a more serious problem. If itching becomes severe, or you develop a rash, see your doctor.

NAUSEA AND MORNING SICKNESS

Nausea is very common in the early weeks of pregnancy. Some women feel sick, some are sick. Some feel sick in the mornings, some at other times, some all day long.

The reasons are not fully understood, but hormonal changes in the first three months are probably one cause. Nausea usually disappears around the 12th to 14th week. Nausea can be one of the most trying problems in early pregnancy. It comes at a time when you may be feeling tired and emotional, and when many people around you may not realise you are pregnant and expect you to be your normal self.

- If you feel sick first thing in the morning, give yourself time to get up slowly. If possible, eat something like dry toast or a plain biscuit before you get up.
- Get plenty of rest and sleep whenever you can. Feeling tired can make the sickness worse.
- Eat small amounts often rather than several large meals but don't stop eating.
- Drink plenty of fluids.
- Ask those close to you for extra support.
- Distract yourself as much as you can. Often the nausea gets worse the more you think about it.
- Avoid the foods and smells that make you feel worse. It helps if someone else can cook but, if not, go for bland, non-greasy foods such as baked potatoes, pasta and milk puddings, which are simple to prepare.
- Wear comfortable clothes. Tight waistbands can make you feel worse.

If you can't keep anything down see your doctor or midwife.

NOSE BLEEDS

Nose bleeds are quite common in pregnancy because of hormonal changes. The nose bleeds are usually short but can be quite heavy. If the bleeding doesn't stop, press the sides of your nose together between two fingers, just below the bony part of your nose. It will usually stop after a few minutes. So long as you don't lose a lot of blood, there is nothing to worry about. Blow your nose gently and try to avoid explosive sneezes. You may also find that your nose gets more blocked up than usual.

PASSING WATER OFTEN

Needing to pass water often is an early sign of pregnancy. Sometimes it continues right through pregnancy, In later pregnancy, it's the result of the baby's head pressing on the bladder.

If you find that you're having to get up in the night, you could try cutting out drinks in the late evening but make sure you keep drinking plenty during the day. Later in pregnancy, some women find it helps to rock backwards and forwards while they are on the toilet. This lessens the pressure of the womb on the bladder so that you can empty it properly. Then you won't need to pass water again quite so soon.

If you have any pain while passing water or pass any blood you may have a urine infection which will need treatment. Drink plenty of water to dilute your urine and reduce irritation. You should see your GP straightaway.

Sometimes pregnant women have difficulty in controlling their bladder. You may be unable to prevent a sudden spurt of urine or a small leak when you cough, sneeze or laugh, or when you move suddenly or just get up from a sitting position. This may be because your pelvic floor muscles relax slightly to prepare for the baby's delivery.

The growing baby will increase pressure on the bladder. If you find this a problem, you can improve the situation by doing exercises to tone up your pelvic floor muscles (see page 13). Ask a midwife or obstetric physiotherapist (see page 55) for advice.

PILES

Piles, also known as haemorrhoids, are swollen veins around the back passage which may itch, ache or feel sore. You can usually feel the lumpiness of the piles around the back passage. Piles may also bleed a little and they can make going to the toilet uncomfortable or even painful. They occur in pregnancy because hormonal changes make the vein around the anus larger. Piles usually go shortly after delivery.

If you suffer from piles you should:

- eat plenty of food that is high in fibre, like wholemeal bread, fruit and vegetables and drink plenty of water. This will prevent constipation, which can make piles worse.
- take regular exercise to improve your circulation.
- avoid standing for long periods.
- sleep with the end of the bed slightly raised.
- use an ice pack to ease the discomfort. Hold this gently against the piles. Or use a cloth wrung out in iced water.
- if the piles stick out, push them gently back inside, using a lubricating jelly.
- ask your doctor, midwife or pharmacist if they can suggest a suitable ointment.

SKIN AND HAIR CHANGES

Hormonal changes taking place in pregnancy will make your nipples and the area around them go darker. Your skin colour may also darken a little, either in patches or all over. Birthmarks, moles and freckles may also darken. Some women develop a dark line running down the middle of their stomach. These changes will gradually fade after the baby has been born, although your nipples may remain a little darker.

If you sunbathe when you are pregnant, you may find you tan more easily. Protect your skin with a good, high factor sunscreen. Don't stay in the hot sun for very long.

Hair growth is also likely to increase in pregnancy. Your hair may also be greasier. After the baby is born it may seem as if you're losing a lot of hair. In fact, you're simply losing the increase that occurred during pregnancy.

SLEEPLESSNESS

Late in pregnancy it can be very difficult to get a good night's sleep. You're uncomfortable lying down or just when you're beginning to get comfortable, you have to get up to go to the toilet. Some women have nightmares about the baby and about the birth. Talking about them can help you. Just because you dream something, it doesn't mean it's going to happen.

It might be more comfortable to lie on one side with a pillow under your tummy and another between your knees.

STRETCH MARKS

Some women get them, some don't. It depends on your skin type. Some people's skin is more elastic. You are more likely to get stretch marks if you put on too much weight.

It's very doubtful whether oils or creams help to prevent stretch marks. After your baby is born the marks should gradually fade.

SWOLLEN ANKLES, FEET AND FINGERS

Ankles and feet and fingers often swell a little in pregnancy because the body holds more water than usual. Towards the end of the day, especially if the weather is hot or if you have been standing a lot, the extra water tends to gather in the lowest parts of the body. *You should:*

- try to avoid standing for long periods.
- wear comfortable shoes.
- put your feet up as much as you can. Try to rest for an hour a day with your feet higher than your heart.
- try to do your foot exercises (see page 13) - these will help.

TEETH AND GUMS

Bleeding gums are caused by a build-up of plaque (bacteria) on the teeth. During pregnancy, hormonal changes in your body can cause the plaque to make the gums more inflamed. They may become swollen and bleed more easily. *To keep your teeth and gums healthy, you should:*

- Pay special attention to cleaning your teeth. Brush really well to remove all the plaque. Ask your dentist to show you a good brushing method.
- Avoid snacking on sugary drinks and foods.
- Dental treatment is free while you are pregnant and for a year after your baby's birth so now is the time for a check-up.

TIREDNESS

In the early months of pregnancy you may feel tired or even desperately exhausted. The only answer is to try and rest as much as possible. Make time to sit with your feet up during the day and

If you aren't sleeping well:
- **Try not to let it bother you. Don't worry that it will harm your baby - it won't.**
- **It might be more comfortable to lie on one side with a pillow under your tummy and another between your knees.**
- **Relaxation techniques may help. Your antenatal class (see page 56) may teach relaxation techniques, or you could borrow a cassette from your library.**
- **A warm, milky drink, a warm bath, some gentle exercise or some restful music before bedtime may help.**
- **A rest during the day can help you to feel less tired.**
- **Talk to your partner, a friend, doctor or midwife.**

accept any offers of help from colleagues and family. Towards the end of pregnancy, you may feel tired because of the extra weight you are carrying. Make sure you get plenty of rest.

VAGINAL DISCHARGE

Almost all women have more vaginal discharge in pregnancy. It should be clear and white and it should not smell unpleasant. If the discharge is coloured or smells strange or if you feel itchy or sore, you may have a vaginal infection. Tell your doctor or midwife. The most common infection is thrush which your doctor can treat easily. You can help prevent thrush by wearing loose cotton underwear.

If vaginal discharge, of any colour, increases a lot in later pregnancy, tell your doctor or midwife.

VARICOSE VEINS

Varicose veins are veins which become swollen. The veins in the legs are most commonly affected. You can also get varicose veins in the vulva (vaginal opening). They usually get better after delivery. *You should:*

- try to avoid standing for long periods of time.
- try not to not sit with your legs crossed.
- try not to put on more weight as this increases the pressure.
- sit with your legs up as often as you can to ease the discomfort.
- try support tights which may also help support the muscles of your legs. You can buy them at most pharmacists.
- try sleeping with your legs higher than the rest of your body. Use pillows or put bricks under the end of your bed.
- try the foot exercises on page 13.

MORE SERIOUS PROBLEMS

SLOW GROWING BABIES

Many of the tests in pregnancy check the growth of your baby. If you have already had a very small baby, or you smoke heavily, the midwives will already be keeping a close eye on you. Regular weighing and blood pressure checks may also pick up signs of trouble. If there is concern about your baby's health the heart rate can be monitored.

In the last weeks of pregnancy you may also be asked to keep track of your baby's movements. Active movements - like kicks - are a sign that the baby is in good health. If the movements slow down or stop it may mean that the baby is not well. You should contact your doctor or midwife immediately.

If tests show that your baby is not growing well in the womb doctors may recommend early delivery by induction of labour (see page 90) or Caesarean section (see page 91).

HIGH BLOOD PRESSURE AND PRE-ECLAMPSIA

During pregnancy your blood pressure will be checked at every antenatal appointment. This is because a rise in blood pressure can be the first sign of a condition known as pre-eclampsia (sometimes known as pre-eclamptic toxaemia or PET). Your urine will also be checked for protein.

If you do have pre-eclampsia, you will probably feel perfectly well. Although most cases are mild and cause no trouble, it can get worse and be serious for both mother and baby. It can cause fits and slow the baby's growth, and be life-threatening if left untreated. That is why routine antenatal checks are so important.

Pre-eclampsia usually happens toward the end of pregnancy, but problems can occur earlier. Rarely, it can happen after the birth. The earlier in pregnancy it starts, the more severe it is likely to be. If it does get worse, the treatment ranges from rest at home or in hospital, drugs to lower the high blood pressure, or occasionally early delivery of the baby.

VAGINAL BLEEDING

Bleeding from the vagina at any time in pregnancy can be a danger signal. You should contact your doctor or midwife straightaway. In early pregnancy, bleeding may be a sign of an ectopic pregnancy or a miscarriage (see page 94), although many women who bleed at this time go on to have normal and successful pregnancies.

Bleeding after about five months may be a sign that the placenta is implanted in the lower part of the uterus (placenta praevia) or that it has started to separate (placental abruption). Both of these can be dangerous for you and the baby, so see your midwife or doctor.

Bleeding may also be due to the fact that veins in the cervix increase slightly in pregnancy and is more likely to bleed, particularly after intercourse. This is known as a cervical erosion and is a normal change that happens in pregnancy. Vaginal infections can also cause a small amount of vaginal bleeding.

Because there are a variety of causes for vaginal bleeding, some of which are more serious than others, it's important to find the cause straightaway.

The commonest bleeding in pregnancy is the small amount of blood mixed with mucus, known as a 'show'. This is a sign of the beginning of labour (see page 80). You should always report this to your doctor or midwife as soon as it occurs.

Other illnesses
You should see your GP straightaway if you have a sudden 'acute' illness - like acute diarrhoea, vomiting or a high fever.

10 What you need for the baby

This is a list of essential items you need to get before your baby is born, and some others that you may want to think about. You may be able to borrow some of these items - and then pass them on later to another baby. Look out for secondhand equipment too but do check that it is safe. Ask your health visitor if you're in doubt.

NAPPIES
(also see page 113)

CHOOSING NAPPIES
You can get **terry towelling** or **disposable**. Each has advantages and disadvantages.

Disposable nappies cost more to use but they save time and are useful if washing and drying are a problem where you live.

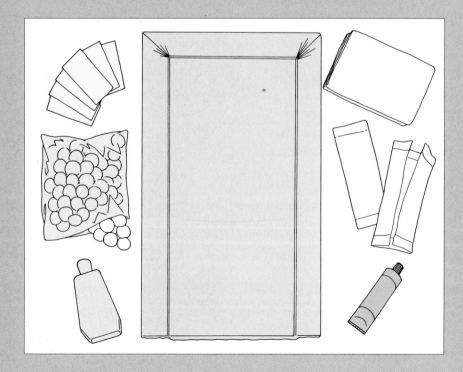

Terries are cheaper to use, even taking into account the cost of washing them. They are more environmentally friendly but the washing, sterilising and drying do mean more work. If you opt for terry nappies, you'll need two dozen - or you'll run out. *You also need:*

- **nappy pins**
- **nappy liners** - either disposable or cloth, which you can wash and use again.
- **plastic pants** - about four pairs, either tie-on or elasticated. Tie-on ones often fit small babies better.
- **bucket with a lid** and **nappy sterilising powder or liquid** for sterilising nappies.

CHANGING NAPPIES
You'll need:

- **cotton wool**. Always choose white. Rolls are cheaper.
- A **plastic changing mat** is very useful and convenient but you can make do with a piece of waterproof sheet over an old towel.
- **baby lotion** or **baby wipes**. Water is fine - and cheap - for cleaning your baby's bottom,

Safety
The safest place to change a nappy is on a mat on the floor. If you use a higher surface keep a hand on your baby at all times in case she rolls off.

but lotion or wipes can be convenient, especially when you're out.

- **baby barrier cream** to help prevent nappy rash - though the best way to prevent this is by changing and cleaning the bottom well and often.
- **a changing bag** to carry all the nappy-changing equipment when you go out. A carrier bag will do but you can get special changing bags that include a changing mat.

BATHING
(also see page 115)

- Any **large, clean bowl** will do as long as it is not metal. Or you can always use the sink but remember to wrap a towel round the taps for safety.
- You also need **baby soap or liquid** which can also be used on babies' hair. Ordinary toilet soap may irritate your baby's skin. It isn't necessary to use baby shampoo.
- **towels**. Two towels. The softer the better. There's no need for special baby towels, unless you want them. Keep the towels for your baby's use only.

SLEEPING

For the first few months you will need a **crib, a carrycot, or a Moses basket.** Your baby just needs somewhere to sleep that is safe and warm and not too far away from you. *You also need:*

- **a firm mattress** which must fit the cot snugly, without leaving

spaces round the edges. The baby could trap his or her head and suffocate. It's best if the mattress has a built-in plastic cover but, if not, you can put a waterproof sheet under the bottom sheet. (Never use thin plastic or a bin liner as your baby could suffocate in the loose folds.)
- **sheets** to cover the mattress - you need at least four because they need to be changed so often. Fitted sheets make life easy but are quite expensive. You could use pieces of old sheet or pillow cases instead.
- **blankets**. Several light blankets for safety and warmth.

Cot safety. Your baby will spend many hours alone in a cot so make sure it's safe:

- The mattress must fit snugly with no space for a baby's head to get stuck.
- The bars must be smooth, securely fixed and the distance between each bar should be not less than 25mm and not more than 60mm so that your baby's head can't be trapped.
- The cot should be sturdy.
- The moving parts should work smoothly and not allow fingers or clothing to become trapped.
- If you use a cot bumper make sure it's well sewn and tied firmly with short strings (no longer than 20 cms).

Pillows and duvets are not safe for babies less than a year old because of the risk of suffocation and duvets can also make the baby too hot. Baby nests' and quilted sleeping bags are not suitable for your baby to sleep in at any time when you are not there, again because of the danger of suffocation.

- Never leave anything with ties - bibs, clothes, etc - in the cot in case they get caught around your baby's neck.
- If you're buying a new cot, look for the British Standard mark BS 1753.

See page 111 for more information on reducing the risk of cot death.

OUT AND ABOUT

Spend some time looking at what is available and thinking about what will suit you best before making a choice. You could always ask other mothers what they have found useful.

- **Baby carriers** (also called slings) are attached with straps and your baby is carried in front of you. Most babies like being carried like this because they're close to you and warm. The back part of the carrier must be high enough to support your baby's head. Check that buckles and straps are secure. Older babies who can hold up their heads (at about nine months) can be carried in backpacks.
- **Pushchairs** are only suitable for young babies if they have fully reclining seats which let the baby lie flat. Wait till your baby can sit up before using any other pushchair.

Before buying anything, check that:
- **the brakes are sound**
- **the handles are at the right height for pushing**
- **the frame is strong enough**

- **Prams**. A pram gives your baby a lot of space to sit and lie comfortably though they take up a lot of space and cannot be used on public transport. If you have a car, look for a pram which can be dismantled easily. Buy a pram harness at the same time as you will soon need it.
- **Carry cot on wheels**. Your baby can sleep in the carry cot for the first few months, and go out with the wheels. It can also be taken in a car.
- **Three-in-one**. This is a carry cot and transporter (set of wheels) that can be converted into a pushchair when your baby outgrows the carry cot.

A shopping tray can be very useful when you're out.

IN THE CAR

If you've got a car, you must have **a safety restraint** right from the start - even coming home from the hospital. It's very dangerous to carry your baby in your arms, and illegal if you are in the front seat. The best way for your baby to travel is in a rearward facing infant baby restraint (carrier) either on the front or back seat. This is held in place by the adult safety belt. Make sure it's correctly fitted. Or you can fit carrycot restraints which secure a carry cot or pram top to the back seat. Always keep the pram or carry cot cover firmly in place. This helps to prevent your baby being thrown out if there is a crash.

FEEDING
(also see page 58)

If you're breastfeeding you will probably want **nursing bras**. They should open at the front and have adjustable straps. Cotton is best because it allows air to circulate. If you try on bras at about 30 weeks pregnant they should fit when needed later.

A supply of breast pads may also be useful.

If you're going to bottle feed, *you will need to get:*

- six bottles with teats and caps
- sterilising equipment (see page 67)
- a bottle brush
- powdered baby milk. Don't buy this too far in advance and remember to check the 'sell by date' on the pack.

CLOTHES FOR THE BABY

Babies grow very quickly. All you need for the first few weeks are enough clothes to make sure that your baby will be warm and clean.

You'll need:

- **six stretch suits** for both day and night **or four stretch suits and two nighties** for the night. **Socks or booties** with the nightie if it's cold.
- **two cardigans**, wool rather than nylon, light rather than heavy. Several light layers of clothing are best for warmth.
- **four vests**.
- **a shawl or blanket** to wrap your baby in.
- **a woolly hat, mittens, socks or bootees** for going out if the weather is cold. It's better to choose close-knitted patterns for safety.
- **a sun hat** for going out if the weather is hot.

Washing baby clothes
If you use a washing machine, don't use enzyme (bio) powders, as they may irritate your baby's skin. Always rinse very thoroughly. Fabric softener may also cause a skin reaction.

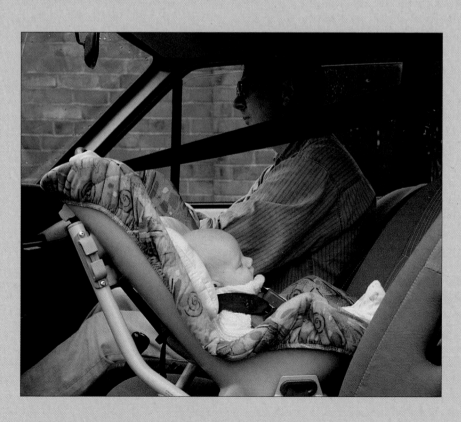

Labour and birth

This chapter describes a hospital birth because that is where most people have their babies but the information will also be useful if you are having a home birth.

GETTING READY FOR THE BIRTH

PACKING
Pack a bag to take to hospital well in advance:

- **front-opening nighties** if you're going to breastfeed and an extra one if you're going to wear your nightie, rather than a hospital gown, during labour.
- **dressing gown and slippers**.
- **2 or 3 nursing bras** - or ordinary bras if you are not breastfeeding (your breasts will be much larger than usual).
- about **24 sanitary towels** (super absorbent), not tampons.
- **5 or 6 pairs of old pants** - or disposables. You'll want to change often to stay fresh.
- your **washbag** with toothbrush, hairbrush, flannel, etc.
- **towels**.
- **change** for the hospital payphone or a **phone card**.
- a book, magazines, personal stereo or some knitting, for example, to help you pass the time and relax.

Many hospitals have a printed list of what to pack. If you're having your baby at home your midwife will give you a list of things you should have ready.

FOR COMING HOME
Pack loose, easy-to-wear clothes for yourself, baby clothes (including a bonnet), some nappies and a shawl or blanket to wrap the baby in.

TRANSPORT
Work out how you will get to the hospital - it could be at any time of the day or night. If you're planning to go by car, make sure it's running well and that there's always enough petrol in the tank. If a neighbour has said that they will probably be able to take you, make an alternative arrangement just in case they are not in. If you haven't got a car, call an ambulance - try to do so in good time.

> **Important numbers**
> Keep a list of important numbers in your handbag or near the phone. There's space for you to write them down at the back of this book. You need to include your hospital or midwife; your partner or birth companion and your own hospital reference number (it will be on your card or notes) to give when you phone in. If you don't have a phone, ask neighbours for the use of theirs when the time comes.

> **Stocking up**
> When you come home, you won't want to do anything much other than rest and care for your baby, so do as much planning as you can in advance. Stock up on basics such as toilet paper, sanitary pads (for you) and nappies (for the baby) and, if you have a freezer, cook some meals in advance.

If labour starts early
Sometimes labour starts early, even as early as 24 weeks. If this happens, get advice immediately from the hospital.

Keeping active
Keep active for as long as you feel comfortable. This helps the progress of the birth. Keeping active doesn't mean anything strenuous - just moving normally or walking around.

HOW TO RECOGNISE WHEN LABOUR STARTS

You're unlikely to mistake the signs of labour when the time really comes but if you're in any doubt, don't hesitate to contact your hospital or midwife and ask for advice. The signs that labour is beginning are:

REGULAR CONTRACTIONS

You will have been having contractions (Braxton Hicks' contractions) - when your abdomen gets tight and then relaxes - throughout pregnancy. Lately you will have become more aware of them. When they come regularly (about every 15-20 minutes), and start to feel uncomfortable, labour has started. Gradually they will grow stronger and closer together.

OTHER SIGNS OF LABOUR

You may or may not also have these signs:

- **Backache** or that aching, heavy feeling that some women get with their monthly period.
- **A 'show'**. Either before labour starts, or early in labour, the plug of mucus in the cervix, which has helped to seal the womb during pregnancy, comes away and comes out of the vagina. This small amount of sticky pink mucus is called a 'show'. You don't lose a lot of blood with a 'show' - just a little, mixed with mucus. If you are losing more blood, it is a sign that something is wrong. Telephone your hospital or midwife straightaway.
- **The waters breaking**. The bag of water in which the baby is floating may break before labour starts. You could keep a sanitary pad (not a tampon) handy if you're going out, and put a plastic sheet on the bed. If the waters break before labour starts, you will notice either a slow trickle from your vagina or a sudden gush of water that you can't control. Phone the hospital or your midwife. You will probably be advised to go in at once.
- **Nausea or vomiting**
- **Diarrhoea**

COPING AT THE BEGINNING

Try to keep gently active if you can. It helps to move around and the time will pass more quickly if you are occupied. A warm bath may help you to relax. Have something light to eat and drink. It's important to keep your strength up and a first labour may take quite a long time.

WHEN TO GO INTO HOSPITAL OR GP/MIDWIFE UNIT

If your waters have broken you will probably be advised to go straight in. Otherwise wait until contractions are coming regularly, about every 10 to 15 minutes, or sooner, or when you feel you can no longer cope on your own. If the journey is likely to take a while, either because of traffic or the distance, or if this is not your first baby, make sure you leave plenty of time to get to the hospital. Second and later babies often arrive more quickly. Don't forget to phone the hospital or unit before leaving home and remember your notes or card.

If you're at all uncertain about whether or not it is time for you to go into hospital, always telephone the hospital or unit or your midwife for advice.

AT THE HOSPITAL

Hospital (and community and GP/midwife units) vary, so this is just a guide to what is likely to happen. Talk to your midwife about the way things are done at your local hospital or unit and what you would like for your birth. If your wishes can't be met, it's important to understand why (see 'Birth plan', page 33).

YOUR ARRIVAL

Take your notes or card to the hospital admissions desk. You will be taken to the labour ward, where a midwife will take you to your room and help you change into a hospital gown or nightdress of your own. Choose an old one that is loose and preferably made of cotton because you'll feel hot during labour and won't want something tight.

EXAMINATION BY THE MIDWIFE

The midwife will ask you about what has been happening so far and will examine you. *She will:*

- take your pulse, temperature and blood pressure and check your urine.
- feel your abdomen to check the baby's position and listen to your baby's heart.
- probably do an internal examination to find out how much your cervix has opened. (Tell her if a contraction is coming so that she can wait until it has passed.) She will then be able to tell you how far your labour has progressed.

These checks will be repeated at intervals throughout your labour - always ask about anything you want to know.

If you haven't emptied your bowels for a day or so, the midwife may advise you to have a suppository or small enema. These aren't always needed. A lot of women find they empty their bowels easily and naturally before labour begins.

Delivery rooms
Some hospitals may have one or two delivery rooms, decorated in a more homely way with easy chairs and bean bags, so that you can easily move around and change your position during labour. Talk to your midwife about this and write your wishes in your birth plan (see page 32).

Bath or shower
Some hospitals may offer you a bath or shower. A warm bath can be soothing in the early stages of labour. In fact, some women like to spend much of their labour in the bath as a way of easing the pain.

Birthing pools have been installed in some labour wards because many women find it more relaxing to labour in water. If labour progresses normally, some want also to have their babies delivered in the pool. If you're interested in this, you must discuss it with your midwife well in advance. If the hospital are happy about this sort of delivery, but do not have the facilities, it is sometimes possible to hire one. Talk to your obstetrician or midwife about the advantages and any disadvantages.

"Gas and oxygen seemed to work for me, provided I used it at the right time. The midwife was really good and helped me with my timing."

"I was really scared about the pain so I chose to have an epidural. It was great - I didn't feel a thing!"

"I didn't want to have any injections or anything, so my midwife told me about TENS. It sounded a bit weird when she told me what it was, but when the time came, it actually did seem to work."

"After the first injection, I felt wonderful, there was no pain and I was on cloud nine. But after the second one, and some gas, I felt confused and out of control, which I think extended the labour."

PAIN RELIEF IN LABOUR

It's important to know what kinds of pain relief are available and to try and sort out in advance what you find acceptable. If your partner, friend or relative is going to be with you during labour, talk about it together. Talk also to your midwife or doctor about pain relief available at your hospital. You can then note your wishes down in your birth plan (see page 32). Don't feel that you have to stick to them if, when the time comes, you want to change your mind.

TYPES OF PAIN RELIEF
'Gas and oxygen' (Entonox)
This is a mixture of oxygen and another gas called nitrous oxide. You breathe it in through a mask which you hold for yourself. You'll probably have a chance to practice using the mask or mouthpiece if you attend an antenatal class.

'Gas and oxygen' won't remove all the pain but it can help by reducing it and making it easier to bear. Many women like it because it's easy to use and you control it yourself. The gas takes 15 to 20 seconds to work, so you breathe it in just as a contraction begins.

There are no harmful side effects for you or the baby, but it can make you feel lightheaded. Some women also find that it makes them feel sick or sleepy or unable to concentrate on what is happening. If this happens you can simply stop using it.

If you try 'gas and oxygen' and find that it does not give you enough pain relief, you can ask for an injection as well.

TENS stands for Transcutaneous Electrical Nerve Stimulation. It's a fairly new method of pain relief offered at some hospitals. It seems to lessen the pain for some, but not all, women.

There are no known side effects on either you or the baby and you can move around while using it. Electrodes are taped on to your back, or occasionally your abdomen, and connected by wires to a small battery-powered stimulator known as an obstetric pulsar. You hold the pulsar and can give yourself small, safe amounts of current.

TENS works, it is believed, by stimulating the body to increase production of its own natural painkillers, known as endorphins. If you're interested in TENS you should learn how to use it in the earlier months of your pregnancy. Ask your midwife.

What you can do for yourself
Fear makes pain worse and everyone feels frightened of what they don't understand or can't control. So learning about labour from antenatal classes, from your doctor and midwife and from books like this, is an important first step.

● Learning to relax helps you to remain calmer and birth classes can teach ways of breathing that may help with contractions.

● Your position can also make a difference. Some women like to kneel, walk around or rock backwards and forwards. Some like to be massaged, though others hate to be touched.

● Feeling in control of what is happening to you is important. You are working with the doctor or midwife and they with you, so don't hesitate to ask questions or to ask for anything you want at any time.

● Having a partner, friend or relative you can 'lean on', and who can support you during labour certainly helps. It has been shown to reduce the need for pain relief. But if you don't have anyone, don't worry - the midwife will give you the support you need.

● And finally, no one can tell you what your labour will feel like in advance. Even if you think you would prefer not to have any pain relief, keep an open mind. In some instances it could make the difference between a painful and an enjoyable labour.

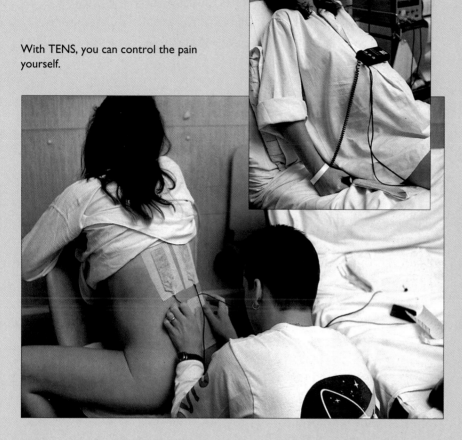

With TENS, you can control the pain yourself.

Injections Another form of pain relief is the injection of a pain-relieving drug, usually pethidine. It takes about 20 minutes to work and the effects last between two to four hours. It helps most women to relax and does lessen the pain, although it doesn't usually do away with it altogether. The drug can make some women feel 'woozy' or sick - or so drowsy that they can't push so well when they need to. Unfortunately, there's no way of knowing what the effects will be on you, until you have tried it. It sometimes affects the baby's breathing at delivery but the baby can be treated if this is a problem.

Epidural anaesthesia An epidural is a special type of local anaesthetic. It numbs the nerves which carry the feelings of pain from the birth canal to the brain. So, for most women, an epidural gives complete pain relief.

An epidural is normally given by an anaesthetist, so if you think you might want one, check with your midwife beforehand (perhaps when you're discussing your birth plan) about whether there is an anaesthetist available round the clock at your hospital.

While you lie on your side, anaesthetic is injected into the space between the bones in your spine through a very thin tube. It takes about 20 minutes to get the tube set up and then another 15-20 minutes for it to work. The anaesthetic can then be pumped in continuously or topped up when necessary.

An epidural can be very helpful for those women who are having a long or particularly painful labour or who are becoming very distressed. It takes the pain of labour away for most women and you won't feel so tired afterwards. But there are disadvantages:

- Your legs may feel heavy and that sometimes makes women feel rather helpless.
- You may find it difficult to pass water and a small tube called a catheter may need to be put into your bladder to help you.
- You may find it difficult to move yourself about to get into a comfortable position.
- You will need to have a drip on your arm to give you fluids and maintain adequate blood pressure.
- You will not be able to get out of bed during labour and for several hours afterwards.
- Your contractions and the baby's heart will need to be monitored by a machine. This means having a belt round your abdomen and possibly a clip attached to your baby's head (see 'Fetal heart monitoring', page 84).
- If you can no longer feel your contractions, the midwife will have to tell you when to push rather than you doing it naturally. This means it can take longer for you to push the baby out. Sometimes less is given at the end so that the effect of the epidural wears off and you can push the baby.
- *Some* women get backache for some time after childbirth.

If you don't want any of these kinds of pain relief, you are free to say so. And if you decide you want pain relief, ask for it as soon as you feel you need it, without waiting for it to be offered.

Alternative methods of pain relief Some mothers want to avoid these methods of pain relief and choose acupuncture, aromatherapy, homeopathy, hypnosis, massage and reflexology. If you would like to use any of these methods, it's important to let the hospital know beforehand. Discuss the matter with the midwife or doctor. And make sure that the practitioner you use is properly trained and experienced. For advice, contact the Institute for Complementary Medicine (see page 125).

What you can do
● You can be up and moving about if you feel like it.
● You may be able to have sips of water but once in established labour you will be asked not to eat anything. This is mainly in case you need an anaesthetic later on.
● If you need the midwife while she is out of your room you will be able to call her by ringing a bell. As the contractions get stronger and more painful, you can put into practice the relaxation and breathing exercises you learned during pregnancy. Your partner or friend can help by doing them with you and by rubbing your back to relieve the pain if that helps.

WHAT HAPPENS IN LABOUR

There are three stages to labour. In the first stage the cervix gradually opens up (dilates). In the second stage the baby is pushed down the vagina and is born. And in the third stage the placenta comes away from the wall of the womb and is also pushed out of the vagina.

THE FIRST STAGE

The dilatation of the cervix. Contractions at the start of labour help to soften the cervix. Then the cervix will gradually open to about 10 cms. This is wide enough to let the baby out. Sometimes the process of softening can take many hours before what midwives refer to as established labour. This is when your cervix has opened (dilated) to at least 3cms.

If you go into hospital before labour is established, you may be asked if you would prefer to go home again for a while, rather than spending many extra hours in hospital. Once labour is established, the midwife will check again from time to time to see how you are progressing. In a first labour, the time from the start of established labour to full dilatation is between six and twelve hours. It is often quicker for later ones.

Towards the end of the first stage, you may feel that you want to push as each contraction comes. At this point, if the midwife isn't already with you, ring for her to come. She will tell you to try not to push until your cervix is fully open and the baby's head can be seen. To help yourself get over the urge to push, try blowing out slowly and gently, or if the urge is too strong, in little puffs. Some people find this easier lying on their sides.

Fetal heart monitoring Every baby's heart is monitored throughout labour. The midwife is watching for any marked change in the heart rate which could be a sign that the baby is distressed and that action should be taken in order to speed delivery.

There are different ways of monitoring the baby's heartbeat:
● Your midwife may listen to the baby's heart with an ear trumpet or stethoscope, or she may use a handheld ultrasound detector. If you want to be free to move around in labour you may prefer this method.
● The heartbeat may also be followed electronically through a monitor linked to a machine. The monitor will either be strapped on a belt to your tummy or clipped to your baby's head (the head can be felt through the cervix and this monitor would be attached during a vaginal examination). Throughout labour the heartbeat will be followed by a bleep from the machine and a print out. You cannot easily move around. Some machines use tiny transmitters which allow you to be more mobile. Ask if this is available.

SPEEDING UP LABOUR

If your labour is slow your doctor may recommend acceleration, to get things moving. You should be given a clear explanation of why this is needed. To start with your waters will be broken (if this has not already happened) during a vaginal examination. This is often enough to get things moving. If not, you may be offered a drip containing a hormone which will encourage labour. If you have a drip, the hormone will be fed into a vein in your arm.

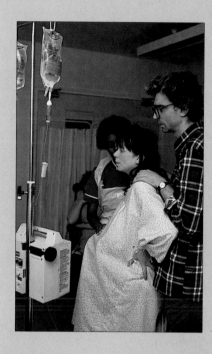

A drip may be needed to help speed up labour - and you can still move around.

Your baby's heartbeat will be monitored during labour.

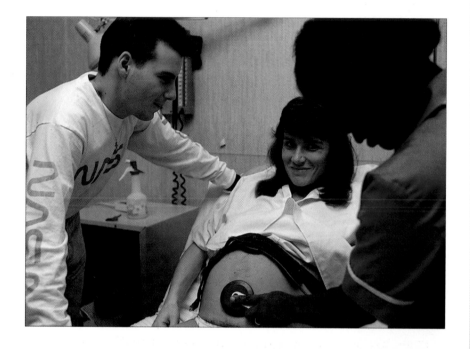

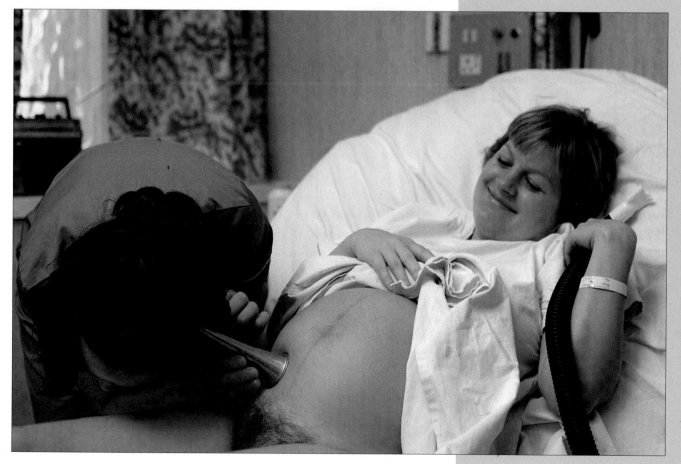

THE SECOND STAGE

The baby's birth The midwife will tell you when your cervix is fully dilated and your baby's head is showing. This means your baby is ready to be born.

Position Find the position that you prefer and which will make labour easier for you. You might want to remain in bed with your back propped up with pillows, or stand, sit, kneel or squat (squatting will take practice if you are not used to it). Kneeling on all fours might be helpful if you've suffered from backache in labour. It's up to you. You should have a chance to try out some of these positions at antenatal classes. Ask the midwife to help you.

Pushing You can now start to push each time you have a contraction. Your body will probably tell you how. If not, take two deep breaths as the contractions start, and push down. Take another breath when you need to. Give several pushes until the contraction ends. As you push, try to let yourself 'open up' below. After each contraction, rest and get up strength for the next one. This stage is hard work, but your midwife will help you all the time, telling you what to do and encouraging you. Your companion can also give you lots of support. Ask your midwife to tell you what is happening. This stage may take an hour or two so it helps to know how you're doing.

The birth As the baby's head moves into the vaginal opening you can put your hand down to feel it, or look at it in a mirror. When about half the head can be seen, the midwife will tell you to stop pushing, or to push very gently, or to puff a couple of quick short breaths blowing out through your mouth. This is so that your baby's head can be born slowly giving the skin and muscles of the perineum (the area between your vagina and back passage) time to stretch without tearing.

Sometimes the skin of the perineum won't stretch enough. Or there may be an urgency to hurry the birth because the baby is getting short of oxygen. The midwife or doctor will then ask your permission to give you a local anaesthetic and cut the skin to make the opening bigger. This is called an episiotomy. Afterwards the cut is stitched up again and heals.

Once your baby's head is born, most of the hard work is over. With one more gentle push the body is born quite quickly and easily. You can ask to have the baby lifted straight onto you before the cord is cut, so that you can feel and be close to each other

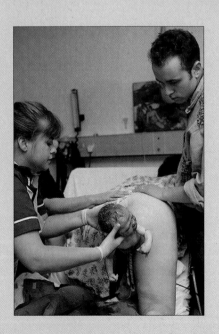

Find a position that's comfortable for you.

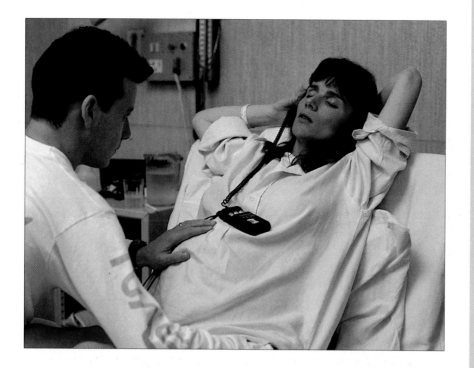

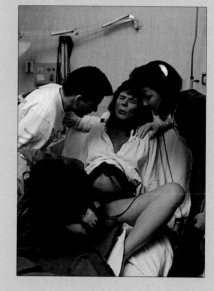

In some hospitals, your partner will be offered the chance to help cut the cord.

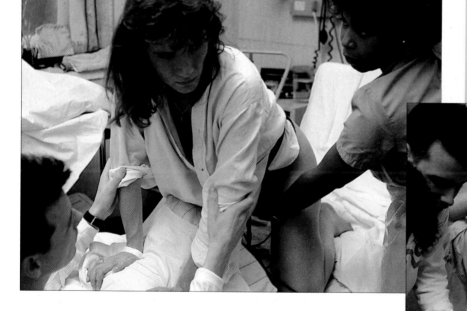

immediately. Then the cord is clamped and cut, the baby dried, to prevent him or her from becoming cold, and you'll be able to hold and cuddle your baby properly. Your baby may be quite messy, with some of your blood and perhaps some of the white, greasy vernix which acts as a protection in the womb still on the skin. If you prefer, you can ask the midwife to wipe your baby and wrap him or her in a blanket before your cuddle.

Sometimes some mucus has to be cleared out of a baby's nose and mouth, or some oxygen given to get breathing underway. This is nothing to worry about and your baby won't be kept away from you any longer than necessary.

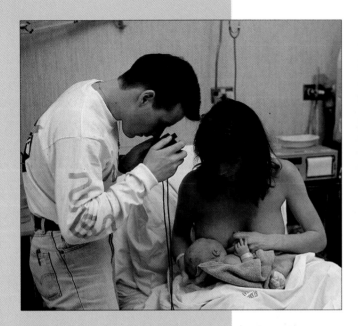

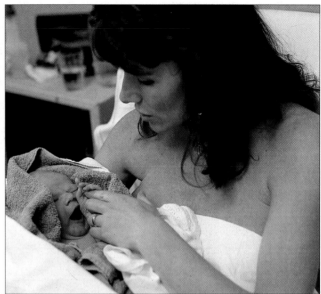

If you're breastfeeding, let your baby suckle as soon after birth as possible. Babies do suck this soon, although maybe just for a short time, or they may just like to feel the nipple in the mouth. It helps with breastfeeding later on and it also helps your womb to contract.

THE THIRD STAGE

The placenta After your baby is born, more contractions will push out the placenta. This stage can take between 20 minutes and an hour but your midwife will usually give you an injection in your thigh, just as the baby is born, which will speed it up. The injection is given as a safety measure to prevent the heavy bleeding which can happen if the womb does not contract properly. Some women prefer not to have the injection as a routine but to wait and see if it is necessary. You should discuss this in advance with your midwife and make a note on your birth plan.

AFTERWARDS

If you've had a tear or an episiotomy, it will be sewn up. If you have had an epidural you will not feel this. Otherwise you should be offered a local anaesthetic injection. If it is sore during this

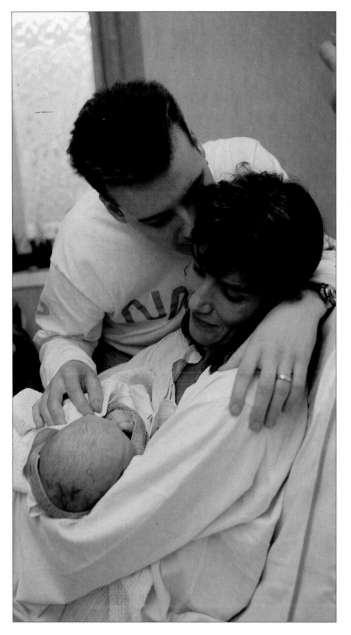

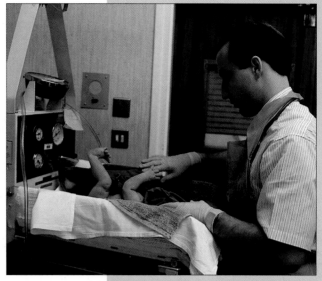

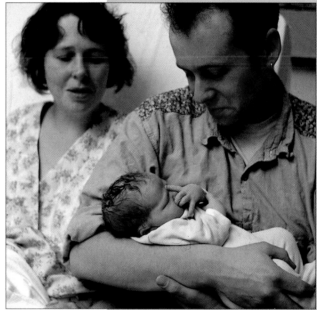

repair, then say so; it is the only way that the midwife or doctor will know that they are hurting you.

Your baby will be examined, weighed and measured, and given a band with your name on it. The midwife will then help you to wash and freshen up. Then you should have some time alone with your baby and your partner, just to be together quietly and meet your new baby properly. If you find this doesn't happen and you would like some time alone, ask for it.

SPECIAL CASES

LABOUR THAT STARTS TOO EARLY

About one baby in every ten will be born before the 37th week of pregnancy. In most cases labour starts by itself, either with contractions or with the sudden breaking of the waters or a 'show' (see page 80). About one early baby in three is induced (see

Hepatitis B
If you have hepatitis B when you give birth, your baby will be immunised to stop him or her being infected.

below) or delivered by Caesarean section (see page 91) because doctors feel that early delivery is necessary for your own or the baby's safety.

If your baby is likely to be delivered early, you should be admitted to a hospital with specialist facilities for premature babies. If contractions start well before you are due, the doctors may be able to use drugs to stop your contractions temporarily. A hormone may then be offered which will help to mature your baby's lungs. If you have any reason to think that your labour may be starting early, get in touch with your hospital or midwife at once so that arrangements can be made.

BABIES BORN LATE

Pregnancy normally lasts about 40 weeks, that is 280 days from the first day of your last period. Most women will go into labour within two weeks either side of this date. If your labour does not start the doctor will want to keep a careful check on your baby's health. If there is any evidence that your baby is not doing well the doctor will suggest that labour is started artificially.

INDUCTION

Sometimes labour must be started artificially. This is called induction. Labour may be induced if there is any sort of risk to the mother's or baby's health - for example, if the mother has high blood pressure, or if the baby is failing to grow and thrive. Induction is always planned in advance, so you will be able to talk over the advantages and disadvantages with your doctor or midwife, and find out why it is thought suitable in your particular case.

Contractions can be started by inserting a pessary into the vagina, or by a hormone drip in the arm. Sometimes both are used.

FORCEPS DELIVERY OR VACUUM EXTRACTION

If the baby needs to be helped out of the vagina - perhaps because the contractions aren't strong enough, because the baby has got into an awkward position or is becoming distressed, or because you have become too exhausted - then forceps or vacuum extraction (sometimes called Ventouse) will be used.

A local anaesthetic will usually be given if you haven't already had an epidural or spinal anaesthetic.

Forceps are placed round the baby's head and by gentle, firm pulling the baby can be born. With vacuum delivery, a shallow rubber cup is fitted to the baby's head by suction. You can help by pushing at the same time. Sometimes you will find red marks on your baby's head where the forceps have been or a swelling from the vacuum. They fade eventually.

An episiotomy (see page 86) is nearly always needed for a forceps delivery.

If you would like your partner - or whoever is with you - to stay, you should ask.

CAESAREAN SECTION

The baby is delivered by cutting through the abdomen and then into the womb. The cut is usually done crossways and low down, just below the bikini line. It is hidden when your pubic hair grows back again.

An 'elective' Caesarean may be recommended in advance if, for example, you have a very small pelvis which might make delivery difficult. An emergency Caesarean may be necessary if you or the baby are at risk in some way and delivery needs to be quick. If a Caesarean is suggested your doctor should tell you why it is necessary and explain the possible side effects. The operation can be done under general anaesthetic, though there is a greater risk of chest infection, or epidural anaesthetic (see page 83). If you have an epidural, you will be awake throughout the operation but you won't feel pain, just some tugging and pulling, and wetness when the waters break. A screen will be put across you so that you cannot see what is being done. The doctors will talk to you and let you know what is happening. Sometimes, if delivery needs to be really quick or when there are technical problems, an epidural anaesthetic may be unsuitable.

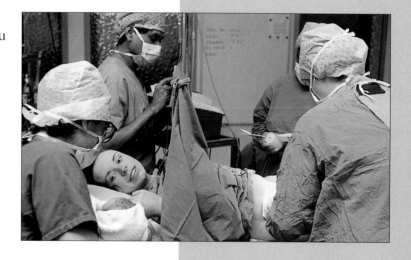

A caesarean delivery under an epidural anaesthetic.

The operation is fast and takes about 10 minutes from when the surgeon starts to deliver the baby. The advantage of an epidural is that you are awake at the moment of delivery, just as you would be normally, and you can see and hold your baby straightaway. Some hospitals are willing to let partners be present at a Caesarean so that they can give lots of support and welcome the baby at birth. Ask.

After a Caesarean you will be uncomfortable for a few days, as you would expect to be after any major surgery. It will be difficult to sit up or stand up straight, and it will hurt to laugh. You will probably have to stay in hospital a bit longer, say about five to eight days, but this will depend on your condition. You will also have to take it easy once you are home. Your doctor will advise you on how much you can do. Postnatal exercises are especially important after a Caesarean to get your muscles working again. The midwife or hospital physiotherapist will tell you when you should begin them. You can also contact the Caesarean Support Network for information and support (see page 125).

BREECH BIRTH

A breech birth is when a baby is born bottom or feet first. This is often considered a reason for Caesarean delivery though it is possible for a baby to be born this way quite normally. More care is needed, especially to deliver the head, and forceps are quite often used (see page 90).

"When she was being born, as soon as they said 'It's a girl', I just felt something. Oh, I thought it was marvellous. I felt love as soon as I knew I was giving birth. I felt something...I felt something special."

"All I wanted afterwards was to go to sleep."

"I kept looking at him and thinking, I've actually got one! He's mine! I've done it at last!"

"It was like being drunk, I felt so special, so full of myself and what I'd done."

"I wasn't elated or anything like that. I think it had all been too much like hard work to feel much after."

a father: *"I was relieved. I was delighted about the baby, but I was more relieved than anything - that it was over, and we'd come through, and everything was fine."*

a father: *"Having seen what she'd been through and seeing him pop into the world, then being together afterwards, I felt proud, proud of the two of them."*

TWINS

If you are expecting twins, labour may start early because the womb becomes very stretched with two babies. More people will usually be present at the birth - for example, a midwife, a doctor, and anaesthetist and usually two paediatricians, one for each baby.

The process of labour is the same but the babies will be closely monitored, usually by using an electronic monitor (see page 84). You will be given a drip in case it is needed later. Once the first baby has been born, the midwife or doctor will check the position of the second by feeling your abdomen and doing a vaginal examination. If the second baby is in a good position, the waters surrounding the baby will be broken and the second baby should be born very soon after the first because the cervix is already fully dilated. If contractions stop after the first birth, hormones will be added to the drip to restart them.

If you're expecting twins or more you may like to contact the Twins and Multiple Births Association (TAMBA), for advice and support. (See page 126.)

WHAT YOUR COMPANION CAN DO

Whoever your 'labour partner' is - the baby's father, a close friend, or a relative - there are quite a few practical things that he or she can do to help you, although probably none of them are as important as just being with you. You can't know in advance what your labour is going to be like or how each of you will cope. But there are many ways in which a partner can help.

Your labour partner can:

- Keep you company and help pass the time in the early stages.
- Hold your hand, wipe your face, give you sips of water, rub your back, help you move about or change position, or anything else that helps and comforts you as your labour progresses and your contractions get stronger.
- Remind you how to use relaxation and breathing techniques, perhaps breathing with you if it helps.
- Support your decisions about, for example, pain relief.
- Help you make it clear to the midwife or doctor what help you need - and the other way round. This can help you to feel much more in control of the situation.
- As your baby is born, tell you what is happening, because you can't see what is going on for yourself.

For very many couples, being together during labour and welcoming their baby together is an experience that they can't begin to put into words. And many fathers who have seen their baby born, and who have played a part themselves, say they feel much closer to the child from the very start.

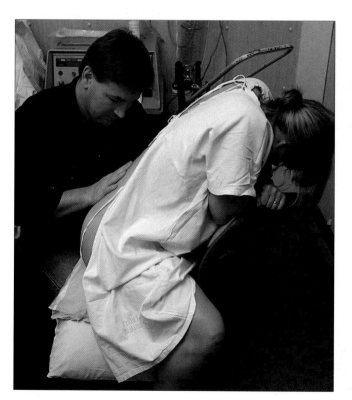

93

12 When pregnancy goes wrong

Unfortunately, not all pregnancies end well. For a few, pregnancy ends with a miscarriage, for example, or with the death of the baby. This chapter describes some of the things than can go wrong. If your pregnancy ends in this way, then you will need both information and support. Talk to the people close to you about how you feel and to your doctor or midwife about what has happened and why. Sometimes it is easier to talk to someone outside your immediate circle. Organisations offering information and support are listed on page 125.

ECTOPIC PREGNANCY

After fertilisation the egg should move down into the womb to develop. Sometimes it gets stuck in the fallopian tube and begins to grow there. This is called an 'ectopic' or 'tubal' pregnancy. The fertilised egg can't develop properly and has to be removed in an operation.

A common cause of an ectopic pregnancy is some sort of blockage in the fallopian tube, possibly as a result of an infection. Warning signs start soon after a missed period. They are: a severe pain on one side, low down in the abdomen, vaginal bleeding, and sometimes feeling faint.

Talk to your doctor to find out why it happened, and whether your chances of conceiving a baby have been affected. Child (see page 125) is an organisation which can offer support.

MISCARRIAGE

If a pregnancy ends in the first six months it is known as a miscarriage. Miscarriages are quite common in the first three months of pregnancy. Probably at least one in six pregnancies ends this way. At this stage a miscarriage usually happens because there is something wrong with the baby. A later miscarriage may be due to the placenta not developing or working properly, or the cervix being weak and opening too early in the pregnancy.

An early miscarriage can be rather like a period, with bleeding and a similar sort of aching pain, maybe occurring on and off, happening at the time when a period would have been due. With a later miscarriage, bleeding is likely to be accompanied by pains that feel more like the pains that come with labour.

If you bleed or begin to have pains, you should contact the person who is giving you antenatal care, either at the hospital or your GP's surgery. You may be told to lie down quietly or to come into hospital straightaway. Sometimes the bleeding stops by itself and your pregnancy will carry on quite normally. But if a miscarriage is going to happen, there is very little that anyone can do to stop it.

After a miscarriage, you may have a 'D and C' - that is, dilation and curettage - to empty the womb. This is done under anaesthetic. The cervix is gently opened and the lining of the womb scraped or sucked away.

AFTERWARDS

One miscarriage will not affect your chances of having a baby in the future. Even after three miscarriages you still stand a good chance of getting pregnant. If you have more than two miscarriages you could ask your doctor to refer you for further investigations.

A miscarriage can be very difficult to come to terms with. You may feel disappointed, angry or even guilty, wondering what you did wrong. Some people fear that the miscarriage may have been caused by making love though this is extremely unlikely. In fact, whatever the cause, it is very rarely anyone's fault.

You will almost certainly feel a sense of loss. You need time to grieve over the lost baby just as you would over the death of anyone close to you, especially if the miscarriage has happened later in pregnancy. Many people find it helps to have something to remember their baby by. In early pregnancy you might be able to have a picture of a scan. After about four months you could ask for a photograph of the baby. If your miscarriage is very late you may be able to see and hold your baby, if you wish, as well as having a photograph. Talking also helps. Talk about your feelings with your partner and those close to you. The Miscarriage Association (see page 126) can give you information and put you in touch with other women who have experienced a miscarriage.

TERMINATION

If tests show that your baby has a serious abnormality you may consider whether or not to end your pregnancy (see page 52). It is important to find out as much information as you can from the doctor about the particular condition and how it may affect your baby, so that you can make a decision that is right for you and your family.

You will probably be very shocked when you are first told the diagnosis by your consultant and may not be able to take very much in. You may need to go back and talk again, preferably with your partner or someone close to you. You will also need to spend time talking things through with your partner or with others close to you.

An early termination, before 12 to 14 weeks, will usually be done under a general anaesthetic. For a later termination you will probably go through labour. You may wish to think beforehand about whether you want to see and perhaps even hold your baby, and give your baby a name. It can make the baby more real for you and your family and help you to grieve. If you don't wish to see

your baby, it's still a good idea to ask hospital staff to take a photograph for you. You may find this comforting at a later date.

You may find your feelings quite hard to cope with after a termination, whether it has been in early or later pregnancy. It will help to talk about them. If you would like to talk to people who have undergone a similar experience you can contact SATFA (Support After Termination For Abnormality) (see page 126).

LOSING A BABY

In the UK about 4,000 parents every year lose a baby because it is stillborn - the baby is already dead when it is born. About the same number lose a baby soon after birth. Often the causes of these deaths are not known.

If you lose a baby like this, you are likely to feel very shocked. But you and your partner may find it comforting to see and hold your baby and give your baby a name. You may also like to have a photograph of your baby and to keep some mementoes such as a lock of hair or the shawl the baby was wrapped in. All this can help you and your family to remember your baby as a real person and can, in time, help in coming to terms with your loss.

One of the first questions you are likely to ask is why your baby died. The doctors and midwives may not know. A post mortem examination may help to find out, although it doesn't always provide the answer. Most hospitals will offer you an appointment with the consultant who can explain to you what is known. If you are not offered an appointment, you can ask for one.

It may also help to talk about your feelings to other parents who have lost a baby in a similar way. SANDS (the Stillbirth and Neonatal Death Society) is an organisation that can put you in touch with other parents who can offer

friendly help. (See page 126 for the address.)

If the death happens before 24 weeks there are no clear legal guidelines and hospital policies vary. However you may well want to arrange a cremation, a funeral, organise a service, or simply put your child's name in a book of remembrance. You should be able to do so. You will need a certificate from the hospital so talk to your midwife or doctor about what you want to do. You could also consult the hospital chaplain, or your own religious adviser.

> **Saying goodbye to your baby**
>
> A funeral or some other way of saying goodbye may be a very important part of coming to terms with your loss - however early it happens. If your baby dies after 24 weeks of pregnancy the hospital must provide a death certificate and arrange a burial or cremation. If you would like to arrange it yourself or organise a service you can do that. Just speak to the ward staff and they will tell you what the arrangements are in your hospital.

13 The first days with a new baby

In the first few days after the birth, you and your baby are beginning to get to know each other. Don't feel you have to make a great effort. Just have your baby close to you as much as you can.

Partners also need plenty of opportunity to handle the baby and feel close. Many fathers feel a little left out, especially if they have to leave you and the baby in hospital and return to an empty home. They may need support and encouragement to get involved but the more you can both hold and cuddle your baby the more confident you'll all feel.

YOU

You may feel quite tired for the first few days, so make sure you get plenty of rest. Even just walking and moving about can seem like hard work. If you've had stitches they'll feel sore and you may feel worried about going to the toilet.

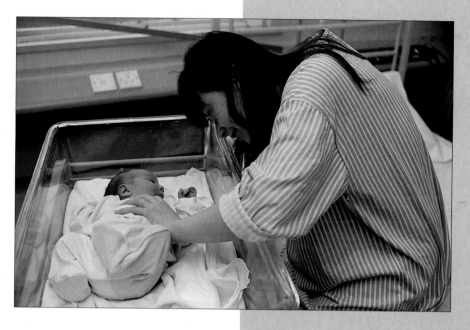

Once your breasts start to fill with milk, they may feel uncomfortable or painful for a day or so. If you're breastfeeding, it will help to feed your baby as often as he or she needs (see page 62). If you intend to bottle feed from the start you needn't do anything, the discomfort will ease after a day or two as the milk stops coming. Ask your midwife for help if you are very uncomfortable.

For a lot of mothers the excitement and the pleasure of the new baby far outweigh any problems. But some do begin to feel low (see page 107), or rather depressed, especially if they are very tired, or feel that they are not making any progress or can't look after their baby as they would like.

When you think what an emotional and exhausting experience you've just been through, it's hardly surprising if you're not feeling your normal self. Some mothers are particularly worried to find that they can't immediately love their babies. As with any relationship, it's not always love at first sight. But this doesn't mean that you won't be able to behave to your baby in a loving and caring way and give him or her the warmth and security that's needed. You may just need to give yourself time.

"I don't think I'll ever forget those first few days. Feeling so happy. Though I don't know why. I couldn't sleep, the ward was so noisy. I was sore. I couldn't move about very well. I missed Alan, and home. But I felt happier than I can ever begin to say."

"I couldn't believe it. I'd never been much of a one for babies. And Dean wasn't even a pretty baby not at first. Very spotty and blotchy. But he was perfect to me. He bowled me over."

"I felt awful. I was so tired, on top of everything else. But there was one thing about it. Bob got to know the baby much better than he would have done if I'd been more on top. He was holding her and cuddling her right from the start."

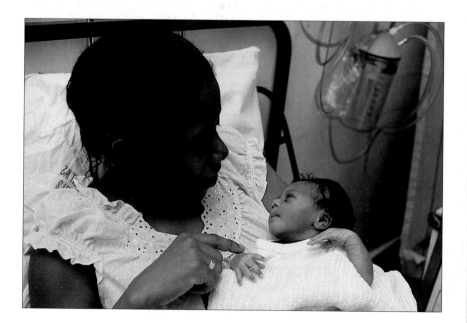

BEING IN HOSPITAL

If you have your baby in hospital, you'll probably be moved to the postnatal ward after the birth to be with other mothers who have also had their babies. Some mothers enjoy their stay in hospital and find it restful and easy. Others find it tiring and rather stressful. It depends on how you're feeling, whether you like the company of other mothers or miss your privacy, and on how the ward is organised. In any case, your stay in hospital, if your delivery is uncomplicated, is likely to be short.

It helps if you've discussed your postnatal care with your midwife during pregnancy so you know what to expect. Any preferences can then be recorded on your birth plan (see page 32) so that staff on the postnatal ward will be aware of your wishes. Some mothers, for example, want to have their babies with them all the time. Others may prefer to have the midwives care for them for the first couple of nights, bringing the babies to them only for feeds, in order to get some rest.

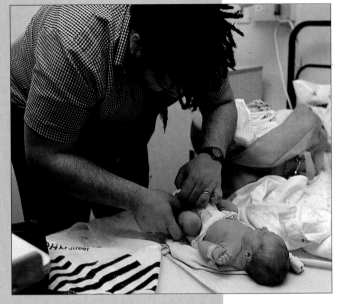

Getting to know your new baby.

You're likely to need quite a lot of help and advice with your first baby. The midwives are there to guide and support you as well as checking that you are recovering from the birth. Don't hesitate to ask for help if you need it. If you do have a problem with the way things are organised in hospital, talk it over with one of the staff. Perhaps a change can be made.

If all is going well with both you and the baby, then most hospitals and units will probably give you the option of going home after 48 hours or even earlier, even if it's your first baby.

The community midwife will visit you at home and continue to help you to care for yourself and your baby. You will need to make sure that your partner, or someone else can be there to help you at home and do the cooking and housework.

STITCHES

If you've had stitches, bathing the area often will help healing. Use a bath or bidet or cotton wool and warm water. After bathing, dry the vulva carefully. Pelvic floor exercises can also help healing (see page 13). If the stitches are sore and uncomfortable, tell your midwife as she may be able to recommend treatment. Painkilling tablets will also help. If there is swelling and bruising, it may be possible to have some ultrasound treatment from the physiotherapist. In any case, remember to sit down gently.

The thought of passing urine can be a bit frightening at first because of the soreness and because you can't seem to feel what you are doing. Sometimes it's easier to pass urine while using the bidet or sitting in a bowl of water. The water dilutes the urine so that it doesn't sting. If you really find it impossible to pass urine, tell your midwife. Also drink lots of water to dilute the urine.

You probably won't need to open your bowels for a few days after the birth but it's important not to let yourself become constipated. Eat fresh fruit, vegetables, salad and brown bread, and drink plenty of water. This should mean that when you do open your bowels, you will pass a stool more easily. Whatever it may feel like, it's very unlikely that you will break the stitches, or open up the cut or tear again but it might feel better if you hold a pad of clean tissue over the stitches when you are trying to pass a stool. Avoid straining for the first few days. Sometimes stitches have to be taken out but usually they just dissolve after a week or so, by which time the cut or tear will have healed.

PILES

Piles (see page 72) are very common after delivery but they usually disappear within a few days. Eat plenty of fresh fruit, vegetables, salad, brown bread and wholegrain cereals and drink plenty of water. This should make it easier and less painful when you pass a stool. Try not to push or strain as this will make the piles worse. Let the midwife know if you feel very uncomfortable. She will be able to give you an ointment to soothe them.

BLEEDING

After the birth you will lose blood and discharge from the vagina. The loss will probably be quite heavy at first which is why you will need super absorbent sanitary towels. During breast feeds you may notice that the discharge is redder or heavier. This is quite normal. If you find you are losing blood in large clots, you should save these towels to show the midwife, as you may need some treatment. Gradually, the discharge will become a brownish colour

"That first week was nothing but problems. One thing after another, first me and then the baby. Everybody was very helpful, but it was still a week or two before I got sorted out."

"I had a lovely rest. No work. Meals provided. Just me and the baby, being together. It was lovely."

a father: *"I'd never been so tired! I spent all my time rushing between the hospital and the flat, catching up on sleep when I could. And the phone never stopped ringing."*

a father: *"It all seemed a bit of an anticlimax after the birth and everything and it felt really funny going home to an empty house. But I knew I could see them whenever I wanted to, so it wasn't so bad."*

Contraception

(see also page 107)

Before you leave hospital, a midwife or doctor will probably talk to you about contraception. If this doesn't happen, you may want to ask. Although it may seem very early to be thinking about making love again, it can be easier to sort out any questions about contraception while you are in hospital rather than later on.

and may continue for some weeks, getting less and less. You can use ordinary pads if you wish but never use tampons as they could cause infection in the early weeks after the birth.

If you're breastfeeding you may not have another period until you stop feeding, or even for some weeks or months after that. If you are not breastfeeding, your first period might start as early as a month after the birth. But it could be much later. You can become pregnant before your period starts, so make sure you work out a reliable form of contraception before you and your partner make love again (see page 107).

YOUR SHAPE

Your breasts are likely to be much larger and will remain so while you breastfeed. You may like to wear a supporting nursing bra if you are breastfeeding. If you are not breastfeeding your breasts will return to their original size in a week or so.

Your abdomen will seem quite baggy after delivery. Despite losing the size of your baby, the placenta and a lot of fluid, you will still be quite a lot bigger than you were before pregnancy. This is partly because your muscles have stretched. If you eat a balanced diet and exercise, your shape should soon return to normal. Breastfeeding helps because it makes the womb contract. Sometimes, because this is happening, you may feel a brief twinge in your abdomen while you are feeding. Breastfeeding also uses up more calories so it can help you to lose some of the weight gained in pregnancy.

Postnatal exercises (see page 105) will help tone up your muscles and help you find your waist again! They will also get you moving and feeling generally fitter. You may be able to attend a postnatal exercise class while you are in hospital or your midwife can show you what to do.

It is quite common after having a baby to find it difficult to hold your water if you laugh, or move suddenly. Pelvic floor exercises (see page 13) will help with this.

RHESUS NEGATIVE MOTHERS (see page 48)

If your blood group is rhesus negative and your partner's is rhesus positive, blood samples will be taken after delivery to see whether your baby is rhesus positive and whether you need an injection to protect your next baby from anaemia. If so, the injection should be given within 72 hours of delivery. Check with one of the doctors or midwives what should happen in your particular case.

RUBELLA

If you were not immune to rubella (German measles) during your pregnancy, you will probably be offered immunisation before you leave hospital. If this doesn't happen, ask. It is a good opportunity to get it done. It's important not to get pregnant again for one month after the injection.

YOUR BABY

Soon after birth you'll be able to look properly at your baby and notice every detail - the colour and texture of the hair, the shape of the hands and feet, and the different expressions on your baby's face. If you notice anything that worries you, however small, ask your doctor or midwife. Your baby will be examined by a doctor to make sure everything is all right. It's a good time to ask questions you might have.

THE NAVEL

Shortly after birth the midwife will clamp the umbilical cord close to your baby's navel with a plastic clip. She then cuts the cord, leaving a small bit of cord with the clamp attached. The cord will take about a week to dry out and drop off. Keep the navel clean and dry until this happens. The midwife will show you how.

VITAMIN K

This is given to newborn babies to potect them from a rare disorder. Recent research has led to a debate about the best way of giving vitamin K. If you want to know more, ask your doctor.

THE FONTANELLE

On the top of your baby's head, near the front, is a diamond-shaped patch where the skull bones haven't yet fused together. This is called the fontanelle. It will probably be a year or more before the bones close over it. You may notice it moving as your baby breathes. You needn't worry about touching it. There is a tough layer of membrane under the skin.

BUMPS AND BRUISES

It's quite common for a newborn baby to have some swellings and bruises on the head, and perhaps to have bloodshot eyes. This is just the result of the squeezing and pushing that is part of being born and will soon disappear. But if you are at all worried, you can always ask your midwife.

BIRTHMARKS AND SPOTS

Once you begin to look closely at your baby, you'll probably find a variety of little marks and spots, mainly on the head and face, or sometimes larger marks. Most of them will go away eventually. Ask the doctor who examines your baby if they will disappear completely.

Most common are the little pink or red marks some people call 'stork bites'. These gradually fade, though it may be some months before they disappear. Marks on the nape of the neck can go on much longer, but they will be covered by hair.

Strawberry marks are quite common. They are dark red and slightly raised. They sometimes appear a few days after birth and gradually get bigger. They may take a while to go away but they will go eventually.

Spots and rashes are very common in newborn babies and may come and go. But if you also notice a change in your baby's behaviour, for example if your baby is not feeding properly or is very sleepy or very irritable, you should tell your doctor or midwife immediately.

BREASTS

Quite often a newborn baby's breasts are a little swollen and ooze some milk, whether the baby is a boy or a girl. Girls also sometimes bleed a bit or have a white, cloudy discharge from the vagina. All this is the result of hormones passing from the mother to the baby before birth and no cause for concern.

JAUNDICE

On about the third day after birth, some babies develop a yellow colour to their skin and a yellowness in the whites of their eyes because of mild jaundice. This usually fades within ten days or so. But a baby who becomes badly jaundiced may need treatment (see page 103).

WHAT A NEWBORN BABY CAN DO

There is one important skill that babies don't have to learn. They are born knowing how to suck. During the first few days they learn to co-ordinate their sucking, swallowing and breathing.

Newborn babies also automatically turn towards a nipple or teat if it is brushed against one cheek and they will open their mouths if their upper lip is stroked. They can also grasp things (like your finger) with either hands or feet and they will make stepping movements if they are held upright on a flat surface. All these automatic responses, except sucking, are lost within a few months and your baby will begin to make controlled movements instead.

Newborn babies can use all their senses. They will look at people and things, especially if they are near, and particularly at people's faces. They will enjoy gentle touch, the sound of a soothing voice and they will react to bright light and to noise. Very soon they will also know their mother's special smell.

14 Babies who need special care

Some babies need special care in hospital, sometimes on the ordinary postnatal ward, and sometimes in a **Neonatal Unit (NNU)**. Babies who may need special care include:

- babies who are born early. Babies born earlier than 34 weeks may need extra help breathing, feeding and keeping warm. The earlier they are born the more help they are likely to need.
- babies who are very small or who have life-threatening conditions, usually affecting their breathing, heart and circulation.
- babies born to diabetic mothers or babies where the delivery has been very difficult may need to be kept under close observation for a time.
- babies with marked jaundice.

Even if your baby is in an incubator, you can still have a lot of contact.

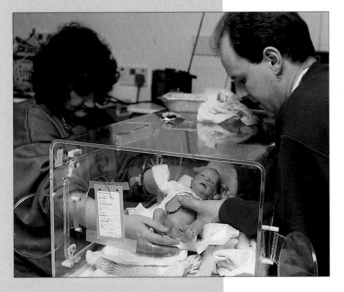

CONTACT WITH YOUR BABY

All babies need cuddling and touching, whether they are in the ward close by you or in a Neonatal Unit. If your baby is in a NNU, you and your partner should try to be with your baby as much as possible. Encourage other members of your family to visit too, to get to know the baby, if this is possible. When you first go into the Neonatal Unit you may be put off by all the machines and apparatus. Ask the nurse to explain what everything is for and to show you how to handle your baby.

FEEDING

Feeding is especially important for premature babies. Those who get some of their mother's milk do better, so think seriously about breastfeeding. Even if you can't stay with your baby all the time, you can express milk for the nurses to give while you are away. Some small babies can't suck properly at first and are fed by a fine tube passed through the nose or month into the stomach. You and your partner can still touch and probably hold your baby. The tube isn't painful, so you needn't worry about it being in the way.

INCUBATORS

Babies who are very tiny are nursed in incubators rather than cots to keep them warm. But you can still have a lot of contact with your baby. Some incubators have open tops but, if not, you can put your hands through the holes in the side of the incubator to stroke and touch your baby. You can talk to your baby too. This is important for both of you. You may be asked to wear a gown and mask. Carefully wash and thoroughly dry your hands before touching your baby.

BABIES WITH JAUNDICE

Severely jaundiced babies may be treated by phototherapy. The baby is undressed and put under a very bright light, usually with a soft mask over the eyes. It may be possible for your baby to have phototherapy by your bed so that you don't have to be separated. This treatment may continue for several days, with breaks for feeds, before the jaundice clears up. If the jaundice gets worse an exchange transfusion of blood may be needed to cure it.

A BABY WITH DISABILITIES

If your baby is disabled in some way, you will be coping with a muddle of different feelings: love mixed with fear, pity mixed with anger. You will need also to cope with the feelings of others - your partner, relations and friends - as they come to terms with the fact that your baby is different. More than anything else at this time you will need to have a person or people to whom you can talk about how you feel, and information about your baby's immediate and future prospects.

There are a number of people to whom you can turn for help: your own GP; a paediatrician at your hospital; your health visitor. Once you are at home you can contact your social services department for information about local voluntary or statutory organisations. On page 125 you will find a list of organisations which can offer help and advice. Many are self-help groups run by parents. Talking to other parents with similar experiences can often be the most effective help.

WORRIES AND EXPLANATIONS
Always ask about the treatment your baby is being given and why, if it is not explained to you. It is important that you understand what is happening, so that you can work together with hospital staff to ensure that your baby receives the best possible care. It is natural to feel anxious if your baby is having special care. Talk over any fears or worries with the staff caring for your baby. The consultant paediatrician will probably arrange to see you, but you can also ask for an appointment if you wish. The hospital social worker may be able to help with practical problems.

15 The early weeks: you

COPING

Going home from hospital can be very exciting but you may feel nervous too, without the hospital staff on call to help you. The more you handle your baby, the more your confidence will increase. Of course, the community midwife, and then the health visitor, and your own GP are there to advise should you have any worries or problems.

INVOLVING YOUR PARTNER

The more you can share your baby's care, the more you will both enjoy your baby. He may not be able to breastfeed but he can help with bathing, changing and dressing - as well as cuddling and playing. He may feel quite nervous of handling the baby and need encouragement. Be patient if he seems awkward at first.

HELP AT HOME

You'll probably need a lot of full-time help at first, not just with the chores, but also to give you emotional support. You're bound to feel up and down and to get easily tired in the early days. Many

women want to have their partners with them so that they will have a chance to get to know the baby properly, as well as helping with the work. It also gives you some time to start adjusting to the changes in your life. If you're on your own, or your partner is unable to be with you, perhaps your mother or a close friend can be there. Even with help you will probably feel tired. Cut corners where you can. *For example:*

- **Cut down on cleaning.** A bit of dust won't hurt.
- **Keep meals simple.** You need to eat well but this needn't involve a great deal of preparation and cooking.
- **Try to space visitors out.** Too many in a short time will be very tiring. If visitors do come, don't feel you have to tidy up or lay on a meal. Let them do things for you.
- **If you need extra help, ask.** Friends or neighbours will probably be very willing to do some shopping, for example.

LOOKING AFTER YOURSELF

REST
When you're probably up at night to feed your baby, and your body is recovering from childbirth, rest is essential. It's tempting to use your baby's sleep times to catch up on chores but try to have a sleep or a proper rest at least once a day.

PHYSICAL ACTIVITY
Continue with the postnatal exercises you were shown in hospital. You'll begin to benefit quite soon if you keep them up and they shouldn't be difficult to fit in during odd moments. Do your pelvic floor exercises (see page 13) three or four times a day. Try doing four lots of five tightenings each time. You can carry on with the pelvic rocking exercise (see page 13), sitting or standing, but don't kneel. Abdominal exercises to strengthen, firm and flatten your tummy should be done three or four times a day:

- Lie on your back with your knees bent up high.
- Draw in your abdominal muscles.
- Curl your head and shoulders from the floor and reach towards your feet with both hands.
- Hold this position for a moment and then lower slowly down.
- Do 10 each time to start with and gradually increase to 20.

Besides these exercises, try to fit in a walk with your baby. A short walk in the fresh air will make you feel good.

FOOD

It's very important to continue to eat properly (see page 8). If you want to lose weight, don't rush it. A varied diet without too many fatty foods will help you lose weight gradually. Try to make time to sit down, relax, enjoy your food and digest it properly. It doesn't have to be complicated. Try food like baked potatoes with baked beans and cheese, salads, pasta, french bread pizza, scrambled eggs or sardines on toast, for example, followed by fruit mixed with yoghurt or fromage frais.

A healthy diet is especially important if you're breastfeeding. Breastfeeding uses up a lot of energy. Some of the fat you put on in pregnancy will be used to help produce milk, but the rest of the nutrients will come from your diet. This means that you may be hungrier than usual. If you do need a snack, try having teabread with polyunsaturated margarine, cheese on toast, sandwiches, bowls of breakfast cereals or fruit.

a father: *"Everybody tells you how much having a baby's going to disrupt your life, your relationships – especially with your partner – but I didn't find that. Obviously, when you're both tired, nerves get frayed, but life's tons better with a baby than without."*

YOUR RELATIONSHIPS

When you bring your new baby home all the relationships around you will start to shift and change. Your mother, for example, may find the change alarming and feel quite unsure of how much to get involved. You may find that she is trying to take you over or that she is so anxious to avoid bothering you that she doesn't help at all. Try to let the people close to you know clearly just how much you do want from them.

Your relationship with your partner will also change. It's very easy in those exhausting early weeks to just leave things to sort themselves out. Take care. You may wake up six months later to find that you haven't spent an hour alone together and have lost the easy knack of talking your problems through. You both need time alone, without the baby, to recharge your own batteries, and time together to keep in touch with each other.

Your relationship with the baby may not be easy either, particularly if you're not getting much sleep. Don't feel guilty if you sometimes feel resentful at the demands your baby makes, or if your feelings are not what you expected them to be. Talk to your midwife or health visitor, if you're upset, but remember, many mothers do not feel instant love for their baby. They come to love them gradually over the weeks.

SEX AND CONTRACEPTION

There are no rules about when to start making love again. If you haven't had stitches you may be eager to share the extra love you feel with your partner. On the other hand, if you're tired and sore, sex may be the last thing you have in mind. Don't rush into it. If it hurts, it will be no pleasure. You may want to use a lubricating jelly the first time because hormone changes may make your vagina feel drier than usual.

It can take some time for the old feelings to come back but they will and, until they do, you may both feel happier finding other ways of being loving and close. If you have any worries, discuss them with your GP or health visitor.

It's possible for a woman to conceive even if she has not started her periods again or even if she is breastfeeding. Contraception may have been discussed before you left hospital and should be discussed again when you go for your six-week postnatal check. In the meantime, you could talk to your midwife or health visitor when they visit you at home, or you could go to your GP or family planning clinic.

The Family Planning Association (see page 127) publishes free leaflets about all the methods of contraception.

THE 'BABY BLUES' AND POSTNATAL DEPRESSION

Lots of mothers go through a patch of what is known as the 'baby blues', often about three or four days after the birth. You might feel very anxious about small things, for example, or mildly depressed, or just keep bursting into tears, for no apparent reason.

'Baby blues' may be caused by hormone changes, tiredness, discomfort from sore stitches or sore breasts or even a feeling of anticlimax after all the excitement. Whatever the cause, you will usually find it only lasts a day or so. Have a good cry if you feel like it, and try to sleep, if you can. The best help your partner or someone close can give is probably just to listen, give you a reassuring hug and look after the baby while you get some rest. If these feelings do not go away it may be that you are simply not

---

Possible methods of contraception

● **The condom.** This may be the best and simplest choice for the early weeks after childbirth.

● **The combined pill.** If you're not breastfeeding, start taking this pill from the 21st day after delivery. If you start it later than the 21st day, it won't be reliable for the first 7 days, so for this time you'll have to use some other form of contraceptive (like a condom) as well. Don't take this pill if you're breastfeeding, as it reduces the milk flow.

● **Progestogen-only pill.** If you're breastfeeding, you may be offered a progestogen-only pill which will not affect your milk supply. This has to be taken at the same time every day. There's no evidence to suggest that this pill affects the baby in any way, but even so some women prefer not to take any form of contraceptive pill while they are breastfeeding and use another form of contraception instead.

● **Cap or diaphragm.** These can be used 6 weeks after delivery. Your old one probably won't fit. Have a new one fitted at your postnatal checkup.

● **IUD (Intrauterine device).** This can be fitted at your postnatal checkup when the womb is back to its normal size.

treating yourself very well. Take time out for treats, however small: a long lazy bath, your favourite food or visit a friend.

Some mothers slide into real depression. They are taken over by a feeling of hopelessness. They may feel angry but more often feel too exhausted to be angry or even to cope with the simplest tasks. If you feel like this you should get help. You, or your partner or friends, should contact your GP or health visitor and explain how you are feeling. You can also contact the Association for Postnatal Illness (see page 127) for more information.

THE POSTNATAL VISIT

You should have your postnatal visit about six weeks after your baby's birth to make sure that you feel well and are recovering as you should from the birth. You may go to your own GP or be asked to return to the hospital. It's a good opportunity to ask any questions and sort out any problems that are troubling you. Routines do vary a little but this is probably what will be done:

- You will be **weighed**. You may by now be on the way to getting back to your normal weight again. Breastfeeding mothers tend to lose weight more quickly than those who are bottle feeding.
- Your **urine** will be tested to make sure your kidneys are working properly.
- Your **blood pressure** will be checked.
- You will be examined to see whether your **stitches** (if you had any) have healed. If you do have any discomfort, make sure you tell the doctor.
- You will be examined to see whether your **womb** is back to its normal size and whether all the muscles used during labour and delivery are returning to normal.
- Your **breasts** may be examined.
- A **cervical smear** may be taken (see page 50).
- If you are not immune to **rubella** (German measles) and were not given an immunisation before you left hospital, you will be offered one now. You should not become pregnant for one month after this immunisation (see page 48).
- The doctor will ask if you still have any **vaginal discharge** and whether you have had a **period** yet.
- There will be an opportunity to talk about **contraception**. If you have any worries over contraception or, indeed, any aspect of sex, now is a good time to discuss them.
- If you're feeling very **tired, low or depressed** talk to the doctor about this.

Babies are quite often brought along to postnatal clinics, so don't worry if you can't find a babysitter. Your GP will probably like to see your baby anyway.

The early weeks: your baby

REGISTERING THE BIRTH

The baby's birth must be registered within six weeks from the date of birth at your nearest Registry Office. The address will be in the telephone book under the name of your local authority (in Northern Ireland, look under 'Registration of births, deaths and marriages'). If you are married, you or the father can register the birth. If you are not married you must go yourself and, if you want the father's name to appear on the birth certificate, he must go with you.

If you live in a different district from the one where your baby was born, the registrar will take details from you and then send them to the district where the birth took place. You will then be sent the birth certificate. You cannot claim benefits or register your baby with a doctor until you have a birth certificate and National Health Service number which will be issued at the same time. In Scotland a birth must be registered within three weeks. This can either be in the district where the baby was born or in the district where the parents live.

CRYING

All babies cry. It's their way of saying that something isn't right. Sometimes you'll be able to find the reason for your baby's distress and deal with it. At other times all you can do is try to comfort or distract your baby. If it's not obvious why your baby is crying, think of possible reasons. *Could it be:*

- hunger?
- wet or dirty nappy?
- wind?
- colic?
- feeling hot, cold or uncomfortable?
- feeling tired and unable to sleep?

- feeling lonely and wanting company?
- feeling bored and wanting to play?

It could be none of these things. Perhaps your baby simply feels overwhelmed and a bit frightened by all the new sights, sounds and sensations in the early weeks of life and needs time to adjust. Holding your baby close and talking in a soothing voice or singing softly will be reassuring.

Movement often helps to calm down crying. Gently sway or rock your baby or take your baby for a walk in the pram or baby carrier or even for a ride in a car. Sucking can also be comforting. You can put your baby to your breast or give your baby a dummy if you wish. But if you do, make sure it is sterilised. You do not need to dip the dummy in honey or sugar to make your baby suck – your baby will suck anyway. Using sugar will only encourage a craving for the sweet things which are harmful to children's teeth.

Some babies do cry more than others and it's not really clear why. Don't blame yourself - or your baby - if he or she cries a lot. It can be very exhausting so try to get rest when you can. Share soothing your baby with your partner. You could ask a friend or relative to take over for an hour from time to time, just to give you a break. If there's no one to turn to, and you feel your patience is running out, leave your baby in the cot, put on some music to drown the noise, and go into another room for a few minutes. Make yourself a cup of tea, telephone a friend or find some other way to unwind. You'll cope better if you do.

If you feel you're having difficulties in coping with your baby's crying, talk to your midwife or health visitor. Or contact CRY-SIS (see page 126) who will put you in touch with other parents who've been in the same situation.

If your baby's crying sounds different or unusual, it may be the first sign of illness, particularly if the baby isn't feeding well or won't be comforted. If you think your baby is ill, contact your doctor straightaway. In an emergency, if you cannot contact your doctor, take your baby to the nearest hospital Accident and Emergency Department.

SLEEPING (see also page 77)

The amount babies sleep, even when they are very small, varies a lot. During the early weeks some babies sleep for most of the time between feeds. Others will be wide awake. As they grow older they begin to develop a pattern of waking and sleeping which changes as time goes by. Some babies need more sleep than others and at different times.

You'll gradually begin to recognise when your baby is ready for sleep and is likely to settle. Some babies settle better after a warm bath. Most sleep after a good feed. A baby who wants to sleep isn't likely to be disturbed by ordinary household noises so there's no need to keep your whole home quiet while your baby sleeps. It will help you if your baby can get used to sleeping through a certain amount of noise. See below for advice on sleeping positions.

REDUCING THE RISK OF COT DEATH

Sadly, we don't yet know why some babies die suddenly and for no apparent reason from what is called cot death or Sudden Infant Death Syndrome (SIDS).The section below lists, in detail, all the advice we now have for reducing the risk of cot deaths as well as other dangers such as suffocation. There are three ways in which you can reduce the risk:

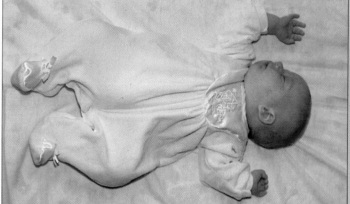

- **always put babies to sleep on their backs.**
- **avoid dressing your baby too warmly or overheating the room (see below).**
- **do not smoke or allow others to smoke near your baby.**

A SAFE PLACE TO SLEEP
Babies should always be put to sleep on their backs unless there is clear medical advice to do something different. Babies sleeping on their backs are **not** more likely to choke and the risk of cot death is greatly increased for babies sleeping on their fronts.

THE RIGHT TEMPERATURE
Small babies are not very good at controlling their own temperature. It's just as important to avoid getting too hot as it is to avoid getting chilled. Over-heating is known to be a factor in cot death. Remember:

- if the room is warm enough for you to be comfortable wearing light clothing (16-20°C) then it is the right temperature for your baby.
- give your baby one light layer of clothing (or bedding) more than you are wearing. If the room is hot for you, keep your baby's clothes or bed-covering light.

- don't use duvets (quilts) until your baby is a year old. They get too hot.
- keep your baby's head uncovered (unless it's very cold) as babies need to lose heat from their heads and faces.
- never use a hot water bottle or electric blanket – babies have delicate skin which can scald easily.
- ill or feverish babies do **not** need any extra bedding. In fact, they usually need less.
- there has been some advice suggesting that it is unwise to have your baby in bed with you. There is no clear evidence of risk but it would be wise not to have your baby in your bed if you have been drinking alcohol, and to be careful not to get the baby too hot.
- babies chill easily if it's cold, so wrap them up well when you go out, but **remember to take off the extra clothing when you come back inside – even if you have to wake your baby to do it.**
- avoid having plastic sheets or bumpers, ribbons and bits of string from mobiles anywhere near your baby, who could get entangled in them.
- make sure there's no gap between the cot mattress and the sides of the cot which your baby's body could slip through.
- remove any loose plastic covering from the mattress which could come off and smother your baby.

CLEAN AIR

Babies should not be exposed to tobacco smoke – either before birth or afterwards. If you, or anyone else who looks after your baby, smoke then don't smoke anywhere near the baby. It would be even better if everyone could make an effort to give up completely. Babies and young children who breathe in cigarette smoke are also more likely to get coughs, asthma and chest infections. For more on smoking, see page 10.

If your baby seems at all unwell, seek medical advice early and quickly.

Do remember that cot death is rare. Don't let worrying about cot death spoil the first precious months you have with your baby.

NAPPIES (see also page 76)

Babies need their nappies changed fairly often, otherwise they become sore. Unless your baby is sleeping peacefully always change a wet or dirty nappy, and change your baby before or after each feed, whichever you prefer.

Organise the place where you change your baby so that everything you need is handy (see page 76). If you're using terry nappies, your midwife or your friends can show you different ways of folding nappies. Experiment to find out what method is easiest and best for you.

CHANGING NAPPIES

You need to clean your baby's bottom carefully each time you change a nappy to help prevent soreness.

- Take off the nappy. If it's dirty, wipe away the mess from your baby's bottom with tissues or cotton wool.
- Wash your baby's bottom and genitals with cotton wool and warm water and dry thoroughly. Or use baby lotion. For girls, wipe the bottom from front to back, away from the vagina so that germs won't infect the vagina or bladder. For boys, gently clean the foreskin of the penis - but don't pull it back.
- You may want to use a cream such as zinc and castor oil cream which forms a waterproof coating to help protect the skin. Or you can just leave the skin clean and dry.
- Don't use baby powder - it can cause choking.
- If you're using a terry nappy, fold it and put a nappy liner inside, if you wish. Pin the corners of the nappy together with a proper nappy pin which won't spring open.
- If you use disposable nappies be very careful not to get cream on the tabs or they won't stick down.
- Put on - or tie on - the plastic pants, if you're using a terry nappy.
- Wash your hands.

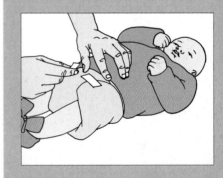

With disposables, the end with the sticky tapes goes under your baby's bottom. Fasten the tapes at the front.

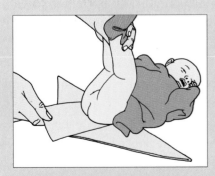

Lay your baby carefully on to a clean nappy and liner.

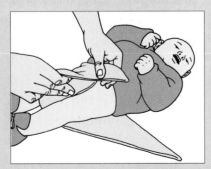

Bring the centre of the nappy between your baby's legs and then bring over the first side piece.

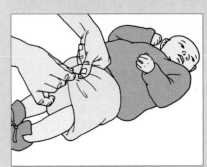

Bring over the second piece and fasten all three pieces together with a nappy pin. Put on plastic pants over the top.

NAPPY HYGIENE

Disposable nappies If the nappy is dirty, flush the contents down the toilet. Roll up the nappy and re-tape it securely. Put it into a plastic bag kept only for this purpose. Fasten the bag and put it outside in your bin each day.

Terry nappies

- If the nappy is dirty, flush the contents down the toilet and rinse off the nappy in the flushing water.
- Have a plastic bucket (with a lid) ready filled with water and the right amount of nappy sanitising powder. Follow the instructions on the packet. Make sure you keep the nappy powder out of reach of small children.
- Put the dirty nappy to soak in the bucket.
- Wash each day's nappies in very hot water. Don't use enzyme (bio) washing powders as these may irritate your baby's skin. Rinse very thoroughly. Don't use fabric conditioners – they may also irritate the skin.

NAPPY RASH

Most babies get soreness or a nappy rash at some time but some have extra sensitive skins. If you notice redness or spots, clean your baby very carefully and change nappies more frequently. Better still, give your baby time without a nappy, and let the air get to the skin (keep a spare nappy handy to mop up) - you will soon see the rash start to get better.

If your baby does have a rash, ask your midwife or health visitor about it. They may advise you to use a protective cream. If the rash seems to be painful, and won't go away, see your GP.

BABIES' STOOLS

Immediately after birth, and for the first few days, your baby is likely to pass a sticky black-green substance. This is called meconium and it is the waste that has collected in the bowels during the time spent in the womb.

As your baby begins to digest milk, the stools will change, probably becoming more yellow or orange. The colours can be quite bright. Breastfed babies have quite runny stools. Bottle-fed babies' stools are firmer and smell more.

Babies vary a lot in how often they pass stools. Some have a bowel movement at or around each feed; some can go for several days without having a movement. Either can be normal.

Most small babies strain and go red in the face, or even cry, when passing a stool. This is normal and doesn't mean they are constipated so long as the stools are soft. If you are worried that your baby may be constipated, mention this to your midwife or health visitor.

What you find in your baby's nappies will probably vary from day to day and usually there is no need to worry about how runny the stools are, for example. But if you notice a marked change of any kind in your baby's bowel movements, such as the stools becoming very frequent and watery, or particularly smelly, or if they change colour to become white or creamy, for example, then you should get advice from your doctor, midwife or health visitor, as soon as possible.

WASHING AND BATHING

(see also page 77)

WASHING

You don't need to bath your baby every day but you should wash your baby's face, neck, hands and bottom carefully each day. You can do this on your lap or on a changing mat. Choose a time when your baby is awake and contented and make sure the room is warm. You'll need a bowl of warm water, some cotton wool, a towel and a fresh nappy.

1. Take off your baby's clothes except for the vest and nappy. Wrap the baby in a towel.
2. Gently wipe round each eye, from the nose side outwards, using a fresh piece of cotton wool for each eye.
3. Using fresh, moist cotton wool again, wipe out each ear but don't clean inside the ears.
4. Wash the rest of your baby's face and neck with moist cotton wool and gently dry. Wash and dry your baby's hands in the same way.
5. Take off the nappy and wash your baby's genitals, again with cotton wool and warm water. Dry very carefully and put on a fresh nappy.

In the first week or so, you should also clean round the navel each day. Your midwife will show you how.

BATHING

Bath your baby two or three times a week, or more often if your baby enjoys it. Don't bath straight after a feed or when your baby is hungry or sleepy. Make sure the room is warm and that you have everything you need ready in advance (see page 77).

- Check that the water is not too hot, just comfortably warm to your wrist or elbow.
- Undress your baby, except for a nappy, and wrap snugly in a towel. Wash your baby's face with cotton wool and water, as described above. Don't use soap on your baby's face.
- Wash your baby's hair with baby soap or liquid, supporting the head over the baby bath or basin. Rinse carefully.
- If you're using baby soap, unwrap your baby and soap all over,

Sunshine

In warm, sunny weather, always protect your baby from direct sunlight with a sunhat. Never leave your baby in a place where he or she could become overheated.

Remember too that a baby's skin burns easily, even in sun that would not affect your own.

What you can do

● You can contact your community midwife or health visitor for advice. Keep their phone numbers where they can be reached easily.

● You can phone your GP. Your GP may be able to advise you over the phone or may suggest you bring your baby along to the next surgery. Most GPs will try to fit a young baby in without an appointment, although it may mean a wait in the surgery.

If you're really worried about your baby, you should always phone your GP for help immediately, whatever the time of day or night. There will always be a doctor on duty, even if it is not your own GP.

still on your lap so you have a firm grip. Take the nappy off at the last minute. If you're using baby bath liquid add it to the water at this stage.

● Put your baby gently into the water. Using one hand for support, gently swish the water to wash your baby without splashing the face. You should never leave your baby alone in the water, even for a few seconds.

● Lift your baby out and pat dry with the towel. Dry carefully in all the creases. If your baby's skin is dry, gently massage in some baby oil. Your baby may enjoy this anyway.

● *Never* leave your baby alone in the bath.

If your baby seems frightened of the bath and cries, it may help to try bathing together. You may like to do this anyway. Make sure the water is only warm, not hot, and don't add anything to the water unless it's baby bath liquid.

ILLNESS

It's sometimes difficult to tell at first when a baby is ill but you may have a funny feeling that things aren't quite right. If you're at all worried, ask for help. You are not fussing. It's far better to be on the safe side, particularly with a very small baby. Trust your own judgement. You know your baby best.

VERY URGENT PROBLEMS

Sometimes there are more obvious signs that your baby is not well. Contact your doctor at once if your baby:

● has a fit (convulsion) or turns blue or very pale.
● has quick, difficult or grunting breathing or unusual periods of breathing, for example, if your baby breathes with pauses in between breathes of over 20 seconds.
● is very hard to wake, or unusually drowsy or doesn't seem to know you.

Your baby may need treatment very quickly. If you can't get hold of your GP at once, dial 999 for an ambulance or take your baby to the Accident and Emergency Department of your nearest hospital as quickly as possible.

PROBLEMS THAT COULD BE SERIOUS

● If your baby has a hoarse cough with noisy breathing, is wheezing or cannot breathe through the nose.
● If your baby is unusually hot, cold or floppy.
● If your baby cries in an unusual way, or for an unusually long time, or seems to be in pain.

- If your baby keeps refusing feeds.
- If your baby keeps vomiting a substantial part of feeds or has frequent watery diarrhoea. Vomiting and diarrhoea together may mean your baby is losing too much fluid and this may need prompt treatment.

If you have seen your GP and your baby is not getting better or seems to be getting worse, tell your GP again the same day. If you become very worried and can't get hold of your GP, or your GP can't get to you quickly enough, dial 999 for an ambulance or take your baby to the Accident and Emergency Department of the nearest hospital.

WHERE TO GET SUPPORT

Everyone needs advice or reassurance at some time or other when they are caring for a young baby, even if it's just to make sure that they are doing the right thing. Some problems just need talking over with someone. It's always better to ask for help than worry on your own. Do talk to your community midwife or health visitor. As you grow more confident, you'll begin to trust your own judgement more. You will be able to decide which advice makes most sense for you and your baby and which suggestions you can safely ignore.

You will also want to talk to friends, relations or other mothers in a similar situation. You'll meet other mothers when you start taking your baby to the child health clinic. Your health visitor will explain where this is and when you should go. She can also tell you about any mother and baby groups in the area. Or your local branch of the National Childbirth Trust (see page 125) or MAMA 'Meet-a-Mum Association' (see page 126) may be able to put you in touch with other mothers nearby.

ENJOYING YOUR BABY

So far we have talked only about the things that have to be done to keep your baby warm, fed and safe. In the first weeks those things can grow to fill all the available time but of course they are only a tiny part of what it means to be a parent. Every second that your baby is awake he or she is learning from you. Learning about what it feels like to be touched gently; about the sound of your voice and your very special smell; about what the world is like and whether it is a safe place to be and, above all, what it feels like to love and be loved.

"You can't really explain, but it's a most wonderful thing to be a mum. To look after a baby and rear her, watching the different little things she does every day. It's just fantastic."

"I think it has changed me. I think I've got a wider outlook on life now than I did before. And I can speak more openly to people. I can speak more freely. I'm more patient, too, whereas before I was very quick-tempered."

"I think there must be something there even before the birth. But it builds up as well. You know, it takes time to form a bond and over the months and years it grows stronger."

"I think if I was to go through it again, I wouldn't look too far forward. I'd just take every day as it came. That's how you get through."

17 Thinking about the next baby?

As you hold your new baby in your arms, it may be impossible to imagine that you will ever have the energy to go through it all again. Or you may be eager to increase your family as soon as you can. Either way, this is the time to stop and think about how you and your partner can prepare for the next pregnancy.

Nobody can guarantee that a baby will be born healthy. However, if you had a low birthweight baby or a baby with a disability or special needs, or a miscarriage or still birth, you may be particularly anxious to do everything you can to create the best possible circumstances for your next pregnancy. You'll want to talk to your doctor about this.

If both parents are in good health at the moment of conception, that is the best start you can possibly give to a new life. There are a few other steps you can take as well.

FATHERS TOO

A father's contribution to pregnancy may be brief but it's still important. A bad diet, smoking, drinking and unhealthy working conditions can affect the quality of sperm and that can stop pregnancy from happening at all.

GETTING HEALTHY AND STAYING HEALTHY

Re-read Chapter 1 **Your health in pregnancy** about diet, smoking, alcohol, and exercise. The advice is even more effective if you start together well before the next baby is on the way. It's a good idea to prepare for pregnancy by taking extra folic acid. Choose foods that contain this important vitamin such as green, leafy vegetables, and breakfast cereals and breads to which it has been added. To make sure you get enough, you should also start daily folic acid tablets containing 0.4 milligrams (400 micrograms). You can get them from a pharmacist. Ask your GP if you want more advice.

THINGS TO THINK ABOUT

Here are some things that are worth doing before your next baby:

- **Rubella** (German measles) can badly damage a baby during pregnancy. If you were not already immune you should have been offered immunisation immediately after your baby was born. If you are not sure whether you are immune to rubella discuss this with your doctor.

- **Long-term medication** If either of you has a chronic illness or disability and has to take long-term medication, talk to your doctor in advance of pregnancy about any possible effects on fertility or pregnancy. It may be possible to cut down the dosage.

- **Diabetes and epilepsy** If either of you has diabetes or epilepsy, talk to your doctor in advance.

- **Medicines and drugs** may endanger your baby's health. Don't take any over-the-counter drugs at the time you hope to conceive without making sure that they are safe to take in pregnancy. Addictive drugs will affect your ability to conceive and, if you do conceive, are likely to damage your baby's health. See page 127 for organisations which can help you to stop.

- **Sexually transmitted diseases** can affect your ability to conceive as well as affecting you. If there is any chance that either of you has been in contact with an STD, it's important to get it diagnosed and treated before starting another baby. STDs, including HIV, can be passed on through:

    - sexual intercourse, especially without using a condom, with an infected person. Some STDs can be transmitted during sex without penetration.
    - HIV can also be passed on by sharing injected drugs equipment.

If you're HIV positive, you could pass the virus on to your baby, either in the womb, at birth, or by breastfeeding. About one in five children born to mothers with the virus are likely to be infected.

> **Difficulty conceiving**
> It can take several months or more to conceive even if it happened really quickly the first time.
>
> If you're feeling very tired looking after the first baby, it may be that you are simply not making love at the right time. Re-read the section on conception to remind yourself when you are most likely to succeed. If, after a few months, nothing happens, and you feel anxious about it, talk to your doctor or family planning clinic.

HAZARDS AT WORK

If you or your partner think there may be a risk involved in your work, talk to a union representative, your employer or personnel department. You have a legal right to know whether there is a definite risk. If there is a risk, ask if you can be moved to a safer job or, if this is not possible, find out whether wearing protective clothing, avoiding breathing in fumes and dust, and avoiding skin contact, is sufficient protection.

18 Rights and benefits

It's very important that you get help and advice as soon as you know that you're pregnant, to make sure that you claim all the benefits to which you are entitled. Benefits have to be claimed on a lot of different forms from a lot of different offices and the situation is always changing. Most of the figures given here are accurate up to March 1995. However, from October 1994 there will be major changes to *statutory maternity pay, maternity allowance, maternity leave* and other employment rights for pregnant women at work.

There are many voluntary organisations that are more than happy to help. Don't hesitate to ask for advice. If in doubt, get a second opinion. See the box below for where to get advice.

WHERE TO GET ADVICE AND HELP

Working out what benefits you are entitled to and making claims can be complicated. Get help if you need it.

● You can go to your social security office (look in the phone book under 'Social Security, Department of'; in Northern Ireland, 'Department of Health and Social Services'). Or go to your local citizens advice bureau (see page 125). Social security offices can be very busy and an advice centre is often the best place to go.

● A social worker should be able to advise you. Phone your social services department (social work department in Scotland, health and social services board in Northern Ireland) and explain what help you want. Some local authorities also have welfare rights officers. Again, phone your social services department and ask.

● The Department of Social Security runs a freephone service called Freeline Social Security on **0800 666555** (in Northern Ireland **0800 616757**). The service does not deal with claims but should be able to answer any questions about benefits.

● Some voluntary organisations offer information and advice on benefits. For example, the National Council for One Parent Families, the Scottish Council for Single Parents and the Maternity Alliance.

BENEFITS FOR ALL

Prescriptions and dental treatment are free during pregnancy, for a year after the birth, and for all children. Ask your GP or dentist for details.

CHILD BENEFIT

What is it? A tax-free benefit paid weekly for each child. It is payable from birth.

Who gets it? Every mother.

How much is it? £10.20 a week for your first child. Other children get £8.25 a week.

How to claim. Claim on the leaflet CH1 which you can get from your social security office. You'll be given an addressed envelope, CH3, to return it. Or you can use the form on the back of the leaflet 'Babies and benefits' which you can get from post offices and clinics. In Northern Ireland, ask for a Child Benefit 'Claim Pack' at a post office or social security office. You need to send your baby's birth certificate (see page 109). It will be returned to you.

ONE PARENT BENEFIT

What is it? A tax-free benefit paid weekly.

Who gets it? Single parents. You can't get it if you're living with someone as a husband or wife.

How much? £6.15 a week.

How to claim. Ask for leaflet CH11 at your social security office.

IF YOUR INCOME IS LOW

INCOME SUPPORT

What is it? A weekly payment for anyone who does not have enough money to live on.

Who gets it? If you're over 18 and neither you nor a partner work over 16 hours a week. If you're 16 or 17 years old, you can claim from 11 weeks before the baby is due, or earlier if you face severe hardship.

How much is it? It depends on the size of your family and your age. If you're under 25 you get a lower rate. The amount will be reduced if you have savings of over £3,000. If you're earning or claiming other benefits, like Statutory Maternity Pay or Maternity Allowance (see page 124), your income will be 'topped up' to the Income Support level for your family size.

How to claim. Claim on form B1 which you can get from unemployment offices if you, or your partner, are signing on as unemployed.

If you're not signing on, get form A1 from a social security office or post office. Return it to your social security office. In Northern Ireland, fill in the coupon in leaflet IS1 'Income Support – cash help'. You can get this from your social security office or post office. Your social security office will send a detailed postal claim for you to complete.

FAMILY CREDIT

What is it? A tax-free benefit for working families on low pay who have children.

Who gets it? Families with at least one child where one parent works 16 hours a week or more.

How much is it? It depends on the size of your family and your income. A couple with one baby can get Family Credit if their earnings (after tax) are less than £150.27 a week. You get less if you have savings of over £3,000.

How to claim. Claim on form FC1 which you can get from post offices and social security offices. Post the form in the pre-paid envelope provided.

If you get Income Support or Family Credit, or have a low income, you may also be able to get other benefits:

MATERNITY PAYMENTS

These are payments from the Social Fund to help you buy things for the baby. You can claim from 11 weeks before the birth to 3 months afterwards. If you can't get Income Support or Family Credit until after your baby is born, claim the maternity payment within 3 months after the birth.

How much? £100. You get less if you have savings of over £500. For every £1 of savings over £500, £1 will be deducted.

How to claim. Claim on form SF100 which you can get from social security offices. Send your form MAT B1 (in Northern Ireland – form MB1) which you get from your GP or midwife. If you're claiming after the birth, send the baby's birth certificate. It will be returned to you.

HOUSING BENEFIT

Housing Benefit will help you pay your rent if you're on Income Support or a low income. It will be paid direct to the council if you're a council tenant, or to you if you're a private tenant.

If you've got a mortgage and you're on Income Support, you can get help with half your mortgage interest for the first 16 weeks. After that, you get all of your mortgage interest paid.

How much? It depends on your income, savings, other benefits and family size.

How to claim. Claim on form NHB1 if you're on Income Support; otherwise get a form from your local council. In Northern Ireland, claim on form NHB1 if you're getting Income Support, which you can get from your social security office. If you're not claiming Income Support, you can get a claim form from your Northern Ireland Housing Executive district office (for tenants) or the Rate Collection Agency local office (if you own your own home).

COUNCIL TAX BENEFIT

What is it? A benefit to help you pay your council tax. Note: There is no Council Tax in Northern Ireland.

Who gets it? If your income is low or you're getting Income Support, you could get Council Tax Benefit.

How much is it? You may get all of your Council Tax paid or just part of it. It will depend on your income, savings, whether other adults live with you, and an assessment of your circumstances.

How to claim. Get a claim form from your local council. If you get Housing Benefit, you will automatically be assessed for Council Tax Benefit and do not need to apply separately.

Note: If you can't get Council Tax Benefit because your income or savings are too high, and there are other people living in your house (but not your partner or a lodger), you could qualify for Second Adults Rebate. This will be 25% of your Council Tax bill. You can claim by getting a form from your local council.

FREE MILK AND VITAMINS

You can get these free if you get Income Support. You get tokens which can be used for one pint of milk a day for you and each child under 5. If your baby is under a year old, you can exchange them at child health clinics for baby milk. You can get free vitamins from maternity and child health clinics if you're pregnant, breastfeeding and for any children under 5.

How to claim. Claim on form FW8 which you can get from your GP or midwife.

121

EMPLOYMENT BENEFITS

If you are, or have been, employed within the last three years, you can claim extra money and qualify for employment-related rights.

If you have worked for the same employer for 2 continuous years full-time (over 16 hours a week) or 5 continuous years part-time (8-16 hours a week), you may qualify for the following benefits.

Many of the rights and benefits in this section will change around October 1994. Some details about these changes are given in the boxes at the end of each section. We do not know exactly how the new rights will come into effect, so get further advice if you think you might qualify.

CHANGING YOUR WORK

If your work is dangerous or illegal in pregnancy (e.g. you work with lead or X-rays) or unsuitable because of pregnancy (e.g. your work involves heavy lifting), you have a right to be moved to another job, provided that one is available.

If there is no other job for you to do, you can be fairly dismissed, but you keep your right to maternity leave and Higher Rate Statutory Maternity Pay, provided you would have met the qualifying rights.

Having time off for antenatal care
All working mothers have a right to have time off work to attend antenatal appointments, including relaxation classes, and parentcraft classes, without losing any pay. Your employer may want a letter from your GP, midwife or health visitor, saying that any classes are part of your antenatal care. After your first appointment, your employer can ask to see your appointment card or other evidence of your pregnancy.

From October 1994 **all** pregnant and breastfeeding employees suspended from their jobs for health and safety reasons will be entitled to be offered a suitable alternative job if one is available. If one is not available, a woman will be entitled to full pay during the suspension period.

UNFAIR DISMISSAL

Under the Employment Protection Act (in Northern Ireland, the Industrial Relations (No 2) (NI) Order 1976) you are protected against unfair dismissal for reasons connected with pregnancy.

HIGHER RATE STATUTORY MATERNITY PAY (SMP)

What is it? A weekly payment payable for 6 weeks.

From October 1994 **all** pregnant women and women on maternity leave, irrespective of their length of service or hours of work, will be automatically protected against a dismissal because of pregnancy or a reason connected with childbirth or pregnancy.

Who can get it? Anyone who has worked either 2 years full-time or 5 years part-time by the end of the 15th week before the baby is due (see chart).

How much is it? It's equal to 90% of your average pay. After the first 6 weeks, you will get basic rate SMP (£48.80) for 12 weeks.

How to claim. Write to your employers at least 21 days before you stop work, asking for SMP. You must send them a copy of the maternity certificate (form MATB1; in Northern Ireland for MB1). Your GP or midwife will give you this when you are about 6 months pregnant. Don't put off writing to your employers if you haven't got the maternity certificate. You can give it to them later. But you may lose your right to SMP if you don't give 21 days' notice.

At the time of going to press the new changes to SMP had not been announced. However it is possible that women with one year's service by the qualifying week will be able to claim the higher rate of SMP from October 1994.

The timings of your rights and benefits in pregnancy is very complicated, so use this chart as a rough guide only. (This table does NOT take account of the new changes to maternity pay and leave from October 1994.)

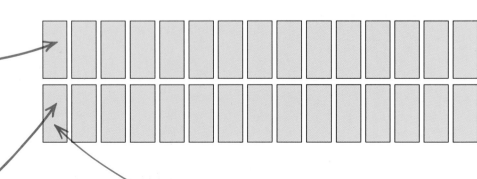

1. In this box, write in the date of the Sunday before the first day of your last period. (If your last period started on a Sunday, write in that date.) Then work along the top row filling in the dates of each successive Sunday.

2. Write in the day of your last period here. Then work along the row filling in the remaining boxes. Each box represents a week. Write in the dates week by week until you get to the date your baby is due.

The first day of your last period.

MATERNITY LEAVE

You have a right to up to 40 weeks' leave and to return to your own, or a similar, job within 29 weeks after the baby's birth. You have to have worked either 2 continuous years full-time or 5 continuous years part-time by the end of the 12th week (in Northern Ireland before the beginning of the 11th week) before the baby is due and must be employed until the end of that week (see chart). If your firm has 5 or less employees, your employer does not have to take you back if it is not reasonably practicable to do so.

At least 21 days before you intend to return, you must write to your employer, with the exact date of your return. Your employer may write to you any time after 7 weeks of the birth asking you to confirm that you are returning to work. You must reply within 14 days or lose your rights. If you are not sure whether you are returning to work, follow the procedure until the final stage and make up your mind when you need to inform your employer 21 days before the date for return.

The length of the leave may vary in these circumstances:

- If you're ill you can delay going back for up to 4 weeks. You must let your employers know before the date on which you intended to return that you will be extending your leave because of sickness. You must send in a medical certificate (a doctor's certificate in Northern Ireland).

- Your employers can delay your return for up to 4 weeks. They must tell you the reason for the delay and give you a new date for your return.

- If there is an interruption of work, such as a strike, which stops you returning to work. If the interruption stops you giving notice of the date you intend to return, you can delay your return for up to 28 days after the end of the interruption.

- If your baby is born early you may lose some leave as you must still return within 29 weeks of the birth.

Maternity leave does not break your service, so the periods of your employment before and after your leave are added together when calculating things like pension rights. This means that if you have qualified for your first maternity leave and have returned to work within 29 weeks of the birth, you will qualify for a second maternity leave at any time. You don't have to requalify. Any general change in terms and conditions, such as a cost of living rise, will apply to you on your return, even if it was introduced while you were on leave.

How to claim. Write to your employer at least 21 days before you leave work, saying that you are going on leave and intend to return. You will be asked for your maternity certificate (form MATB1; in Northern Ireland form MB1) which your GP, midwife or health visitor will give you. If you have to go into hospital before writing your letter, just write as soon as you can.

> From October 1994 **all** pregnant women will be entitled to 14 weeks' maternity leave and the right to go back to their jobs. During the 14 weeks all contractual benefits apart from pay will continue to accrue. An employee must inform her employer in writing at least 21 days before the maternity leave starts that she is pregnant and the expected week of childbirth.

If you have worked for the same employer for 2 continuous years full-time (over 16 hours a week) or 5 continuous years part-time (8-16 hours a week), you may qualify for the following benefits:

UNFAIR DISMISSAL

Although you don't have an automatic right to protection against dismissal for reasons of pregnancy you may be able to get compensation for sex discrimination through an industrial tribunal, if your employer sacks you just because you are pregnant. Contact your trade union or the Equal Opportunities Commission (see page 125).

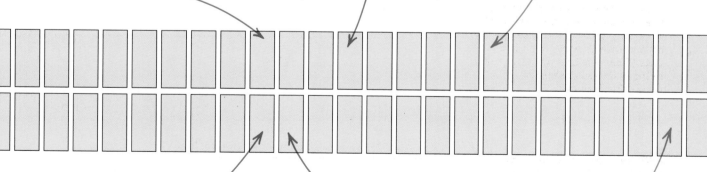

If you are taking maximum maternity leave, you should have written to your employer by now to say so, and to say whether you intend to return to work after the birth.

If you are getting maternity allowance or statutory maternity pay, this is the earliest they can start. If you want to keep your right to return to work, this is the earliest you can leave work.

If you qualify for maternity allowance or statutory maternity pay, you should have stopped working by now if you want the maximum 18 weeks' payment.

If you qualify for maternity allowance, claim it as soon as possible.

If you qualify for maternity payment from the social fund, claim it as soon as possible.

The date your baby is due.

From October 1994 **all** pregnant women and women on maternity leave with **less** than two years service full-time or five years service part-time will be automatically protected against dismissal for reasons of pregnancy or childbirth.

STATUTORY MATERNITY PAY

What is it? A weekly allowance. It can be paid for any 18-week period between week 11 before the birth and week 11 after the birth. Week 11 before the birth is the earliest you can get SMP. You can work later in your pregnancy if you wish. But for every week that you work after week 7 before the birth, you will lose one week's SMP. For example, if you work in week 6 and start getting SMP in week 5, you can only get SMP for 17 weeks. Your first 6 weeks will always be paid at the higher rate if you qualify. The SMP is paid by your employer and then reclaimed from the government.

Who gets it? You must earn on average over £57 a week and have been working with the same employer for at least 26 weeks, by the 15th week before your baby is due.

How much is it? £48.80 a week.

How to claim. Write to your employer at least 21 days before you stop work. You must send form MATB1 (in Northern Ireland, form MB1) which you can get from your GP or midwife. If you don't have the form, write anyway and send the form later.

At the time of going to press the new changes to SMP had not been announced. However, from October 1994, it is likely that the amount of SMP will be slightly increased and you may have to have worked less time with your employer to qualify. Check with your employer, trade union or advice agency for details.

MATERNITY ALLOWANCE

What is it? A weekly allowance for working women who cannot get SMP (see left). It is paid for 18 weeks through an order book at the post office. You start cashing vouchers at the post office from the 11th week before the baby is due. If you work later than the 7th week, you will lose your allowance for any weeks worked.

Who gets it? Anyone, employed or self employed, who has worked and paid full rate National Insurance for at least 26 weeks out of the last 52 weeks, ending with the 15th week before the baby is due, can claim it. If you failed to give your 21 days' notice for SMP you may be able to claim some Maternity Allowance.

How much is it? £44.55.

How to claim. Claim with form MA1 which you can get from your antenatal clinic or social security office, and form MATB1 (in Northern Ireland form MB1) which you get from your GP or midwife. If your employer has turned you down for SMP, ask for SMP1 from your employer and send that too. Claim as soon as possible after the 26th week of pregnancy. Don't put off sending it in because you are waiting for MATB1 or SMP1. You can send them later.

From October 1994 the amount of maternity allowance may be increased for some women. Check with your local social security office for details.

WOMEN WHO HAVE PAID NATIONAL INSURANCE

SICKNESS BENEFIT

This is a weekly benefit which is paid from 6 weeks before the birth until 2 weeks after the birth.

Who gets it? If you can't get SMP or Maternity Allowance but you have worked and paid National Insurance in the last 3 years, you may be able to claim this benefit.

How much is it? £43.45.

How to claim. Ask your social security officer to check whether you're eligible for Sickness Benefit and claim as you would for Maternity Allowance.

PROBLEMS

If you have problems getting any of the employment rights listed above, get advice from your trade union, citizens advice bureau, local law centre or the Maternity Alliance (address on page 125). You may be able to appeal.

The timing of your rights and benefits in pregnancy is very complicated, so use this weekly chart as a rough guide only.

Claim child benefit as soon as you have registered your baby's birth and have the birth certificate.

By this week your employer must receive your reply confirming your intention to return.

If you are taking maximum time off work, you must return to work before the end of this week.

week

| 1 | 2 | 3 | 4 | 5 | 6 | 7 | 8 | 9 | 10 | 11 | 12 | 13 | 14 | 15 | 16 | 17 | 18 | 19 | 20 | 21 | 22 | 23 | 24 | 25 | 26 | 27 | 28 |

The week your baby is born.

If you qualify for maternity payment from the social fund you must apply by now.

Your employer may write to you asking you to confirm your intention to return to work.

If you haven't already told your employer when you are returning to work, you must do so by now.

USEFUL ORGANISATIONS

Some of these organisations are large. Many are small. Some offer advice or information face to face or over the telephone. Others concentrate on providing useful leaflets or books. Many have local branches or can put you in touch with local groups or a local contact.

Where there are separate addresses for the same or similar organisations in Scotland, Wales and Northern Ireland, these are given. If the UK is not covered by one or more organisations the area covered is indicated by 'E' – England only, 'W' – Wales, 'NI' – Northern Ireland, 'S' – Scotland. If you live in Wales you can contact Health Link Wales (0800) 665544 for information on local groups.

Organisations marked * produce publications. When you write for information it's important to remember to enclose a large stamped addressed envelope for a reply. Many organisations are run by volunteers and nearly all have a very tight budget.

SUPPORT AND INFORMATION

ACAS (Advisory, Conciliation and Arbitration Service) (E, S & W)
Clifton House
83 Euston Square
London NW1 2RB
(071) 396 5100
Advice on time off for antenatal care and on matters like unfair dismissal. For your nearest office, look in the phone book or ask at your local library or citizens advice bureau.*

Association of Breastfeeding Mothers
26 Herschell Close
London SE26 4TH
(081) 778 4769
Telephone advice service for breastfeeding mothers and those wanting to breastfeed. Runs support groups (babies welcome). Help given to those wishing to set up a group in their area.*

Association for Improvements in the Maternity Services (AIMS)
40 Kingswood Avenue
London NW6 6LS
(081) 960 5585
In Scotland:
40 Leamington Terrace
Edinburgh EH10 4JL
(031) 229 6259
Voluntary pressure group which aims for improvements in maternity services. Support and advice about parents' rights, complaints procedures and choices within maternity care, including home birth.*

British Diabetic Association
10 Queen Anne Street
London W1M 0BD
(071) 323 1531
In Northern Ireland:
31 Grange Park
Belfast BT17 0AN
(0232) 610630/381213
National charity offering information and support through a network of local groups to people with diabetes and their families.*

Caesarean Support Network
c/o Sheila Tunstall
2 Hurst Park Drive
Huyton
Liverpool L36 1TF
(051) 480 1184
Offers emotional support and practical advice to mothers who have had or may need a caesarean delivery. Can put you in touch with a local mother who has undergone a caesarean and understands the problems.*

Child
PO Box 154
Hounslow TW5 0EZ
(081) 893 7110
Self-help organisation offering information and support to people coping with problems of infertility and childlessness. Telephone helplines for general problems and special helplines for specific problems like IVF, GIFT, ectopic pregnancies, miscarriages, still births, endometriosis, polycystic ovaries and adoption. May be able to put you in touch with a local contact or group.*

Child Poverty Action Group (CPAG)
4th Floor
1-5 Bath Street
London EC1V 9PY
(071) 253 3406
In Northern Ireland:
9 Clarendon Street
Londonderry BT48 7EP
(0504) 267777
Information on welfare benefits.*

Citizens Advice Bureaux (CABs)
Information and advice on topics including benefits, maternity rights, debts, housing, consumer, employment and legal problems as well as family and personal difficulties. Have details of useful national and local organisations. Free and confidential. Opening times vary. Ask for the address at your local library or look in your phone book.*

Community Health Councils (CHCs)
(Local Health Councils in Scotland; authority/local Health and Social Services Councils in NU) Represent the interests of consumers in the NHS. Can advise you on local NHS services and your entitlements and help you if you are having difficulties or wish to make a complaint. Have information on other local organisations. Look in the phone book under your health authority/health board/local helath and Social Services Board.

Equal Opportunities Commission
Overseas House
Quay Street
Manchester M3 3HN
(061) 833 9244
Information and advice on issues of discrimination and equal opportunities.*

Family Health Services Authorities (FHSAs)
These have replaced Family Practitioner Committees. If you're new to an area they can give you a list of local doctors including those with a special interest in pregnancy and childbirth. If you have difficulty in finding a GP to take you on, contact the FHSA. Look in the phone book under the name of your local health authority/health board.
In Northern Ireland:
Central Services Agency for Health and Personal Social Services (CSA)
25 Adelaide Street
Belfast BT2 8FD
(0232) 324431

Family Welfare Association
501-505 Kingsland Road
London E8 4AU
(071) 254 6251
National charity providing free social work services, e.g. counselling for relationship difficulties and advice on benefits, housing and other problems. Provides grants for people in need throughout the UK.*

Health Link Wales/Cadwyn Iach Cymru (W)
Health Promotion Wales
Ffynnon-las
Ty Glas Avenue
Llanishen
Cardiff CF4 5DZ
(0800) 665544
Information on local self-help groups in Wales.*

Health Search Scotland (S)
Woodburn House
Canaan Lane
Edinburgh EH10 4SG
(031) 452 8666
Information on voluntary organisations and local self-help groups in Scotland.*

Independent Midwives Association
Nightingale Cottage
Shamblehurst Lane
Botley
Hampshire SO3 2BY
(0703) 694429
Free advice to women thinking about a home birth. Offers full care to women who book with them for home births. Fees vary.*

Institute for Complementary Medicine
PO Box 194
London SE16 1QZ
(071) 237 5165
Charity providing information on complementary medicine and referrals to qualified practitioners or helpful organisations.*

La Leche League (Great Britain)
BM 3424
London WC1N 3XX
(071) 242 1278 24-hour answerphone
Help and information for women wanting to breastfeed their babies and personal counselling to mothers having problems in breastfeeding. Local groups hold friendly, informal discussions on breastfeeding, birth and parenthood.*

Labour Relations Agency (NI)
Windsor House
9-15 Bedford Street
Belfast BT2 7NU
(0232) 321442
Advice on maternity rights in Northern Ireland.*

Life
Life House
Newbold Terrace
Leamington Spa
Warwicks. CV32 4EA
(0926) 421587
Charity offering information and advice on pregnancy, abortion, miscarriage and stillbirth.*

Local advice agencies.
There may be a number of helpful local advice agencies in your district offering general advice on a range of topics, like benefits, debts and consumer problems, or specialising in one area such as law or housing. To find out what exists ask at your library or town hall.

Maternity Alliance
15 Britannia Street
London WC1X 9JP
(071) 837 1265
Information on all aspects of maternity services, rights at work and benefits for families.*

National Association for Maternal and Child Welfare
1st Floor
40-42 Osnaburgh Street
London NW1 3ND
(071) 383 4115
Telephone advice on childcare and family life.*

National Childbirth Trust (NCT)
Alexandra House
Oldham Terrace
London W3 6NH
(081) 992 8637
National charity with branches throughout the UK. Runs antenatal classes giving information on labour and methods of relaxation, with breathing and massage and details of different birth positions. Also offers help with breastfeeding. Informal support from other mothers. Provides information for parents with disabilities or medical conditions and puts them in touch with each other. Local branches.*

National Society for the Prevention of Cruelty to Children (NSPCC)
67 Saffron Hill
London EC1N 8RS
(071) 242 1626
Aims to prevent all forms of child abuse. If you're in need of help or know of anyone who needs help, look in the phone book for your nearest NSPCC office.*
In Northern Ireland:
National Society for the Prevention of Cruelty to Children (NSPCC)
16 Rosemary Street
Belfast BT1 1QD
(0232) 240311
A 24-hour service to protect children from abuse and neglect. Offers practical help to parents experiencing difficulties with their children.*

Northern Ireland Housing Executive
1 May Street
Belfast BT1 4NA
Offers advice and information on all aspects of housing.

Northern Ireland Marriage Guidance Council (Relate)
76 Dublin Road
Belfast BT2 7HP
(0232) 323454
A confidential counselling service for people with relationship problems of any kind.

Patients' Association
18 Victoria Park Square
Bethnal Green
London E2 9PF
(081) 981 5676
Advice service for patients who have difficulties with their doctor.*

Public libraries
Useful starting points for finding out addresses of national and local organisations. Librarians are usually helpful in producing information or in pointing you in the right direction.

Relate: Marriage Guidance
Herbert Gray College
Little Church Street
Rugby CV21 3AP
(0788) 573241
Confidential counselling on relationship problems of any kind. Look in the phone book for your local branch under 'Relate' or 'Marriage guidance' or contact the above address.*

Shelter, the National Campaign for the Homeless
88 Old Street
London EC1V 9HU
(071) 253 0202
In Northern Ireland:
165 University Street
Belfast BT7 1HR
(0232) 247752
In Wales:
Shelter Wales/Shelter Cymru
25 Walter Road
Swansea
W. Glamorgan SA1 5NN
(0792) 469400
Information and advice on housing matters, including tenants' rights, welfare rights, how to claim improvement grants, etc. If you have housing difficulties, seek advice as soon as possible. Accommodation law is very complex and you could be jeopardising your chances of finding a suitable home. Contact for details of your local Shelter Housing Aid Centre.*

Social Security: Freeline
For general advice on all social security benefits, pensions and national insurance including maternity benefits and Income Support, phone Freeline Social Security on 0800 666555 between 8.30 am and 5 pm on weekdays. Calls are free. There is an answerphone service out of hours.

Advice in Gujerati, Urdu or Punjabi:
Phone Freeline 0800 289188 between 9 am and 4 pm weekdays. For Punjabi only telephone Freeline 0800 521360 during the same hours.

In Northern Ireland:
Phone Freeline Social Security (Northern Ireland) on 0800 616757 for advice between 9 am and 4.30 pm on weekdays.

Social security: local offices
For general advice on all social

security benefits, pensions and National Insurance, including maternity benefits and Income Support, telephone, write or call in to your local social security office. The address will be in the phone book under 'social security'. Hours are usually 9.30 am to 3.30 pm. In busy offices there may be a very long wait if you call in.

Social services
A social worker at your local social services area office will give you information on topics including benefits, housing, financial difficulties, employment, relationship problems, childcare and useful organisations. Look up social services in the phone book under the name of your local authority or ask at your local library. Phone, write or call in.

There may also be a social worker based at the hospital whom you could talk to either during your antenatal care or when you or your baby are in hospital. Ask your midwife or other hospital staff to put you in contact.

Society to Support Home Confinements
'Lydgate'
Wolsingham
Co Durham DL13 3HA
(0388) 528044 preferably after 6 pm
Voluntary organisation helping women who want to give birth at home but are meeting with difficulties. Telephone support.

Twins and Multiple Births Association
(TAMBA)
PO Box 30
Little Sutton
S. Wirral L66 1TH
(051) 348 0020
TAMBA Twinline (helpline) 0732 868000
6 pm-11 pm weekdays; 8 am-11 pm weekends
In Northern Ireland:
Christina Angus
1 Erindee Avenue
Donaghadee BT21 0NE
(0247) 888757
Self-help organisation to encourage and support parents of twins, triplets or more. Will put parents in touch with local support groups, or specialist groups for parents of triplets or more, parents of children with special needs or bereaved parents, if appropriate.*

Women's Aid Federation
PO Box 391
Bristol BS99 7WS
(0272) 633542
In Northern Ireland:
Women's Aid Federation
129 University Street
Belfast BT7 1HP
(0232) 249041
In Scotland:
Scottish Women's Aid
13/9 North Bank Street
Edinburgh EH1 2LP
(031) 225 8011
In Wales:
Welsh Women's Aid
38/48 Crwys Road
Cardiff CF2 4NN
(0222) 390874/878
Advice, support and refuge to women who have been abused mentally, physically or sexually, and their children. Local groups.*

COPING ALONE

CRY-SIS (E, W & NI)
BM CRY-SIS
LONDON WC1N 3XX
(071) 404 5011

In Scotland:
CRY-SIS
21 Falkland Gardens
Edinburgh EH12 6UW
(031) 334 5317
Help and support for parents whose children cry excessively, have a sleep problem or have temper tantrums and other behaviour difficulties. Local voluntary counsellors who have experienced the same difficulties.*

Gingerbread
35 Wellington Street
London WC2E 7BB
(071) 240 0953
In Scotland:
Gingerbread Scotland
304 Maryhill Road
Glasgow G20 7YE
(041) 353 0953
In Northern Ireland:
Gingerbread Northern Ireland
169 University Street
Belfast BT7 1HR
(0232) 231417
In Wales:
Gingerbread Wales
Room 16
Albion Chambers
Swansea
W. Glamorgan SA1 1RN
(0792) 648728
Self-help associations for one parent families. A network of local groups offers mutual support, friendship, information, advice and practical help. Do get in touch if you are pregnant and on your own.*

MAMA (Meet-a-mum) Association
c/o Briony Hallam
58 Malden Avenue
S. Norwood
London SE25 4HS
(081) 656 7318
Support for mothers suffering from postnatal depression or who feel lonely and isolated looking after a child at home. Will try to put you in touch with another mother who has experienced similar problems, with a group of mothers locally, or help you to find ways of meeting people.*

National Council for One Parent Families
(E, W & NI)
255 Kentish Town Road
London NW5 2LX
(071) 267 1361 (not Wednesdays)
In Scotland:
Scottish Council for Single Parents
13 Gayfield Square
Edinburgh EH1 3NX
(031) 556 3899
Information on benefits and employment rights in pregnancy, social security, taxation, housing problems and maintenance.*

Parentline (E & NI)
Westbury House
57 Hart Road
Thundersley
Essex SS7 3PD
(0268) 757007
Voluntary self-help organisation offering confidential support to parents under stress. A network of local telephone helplines is manned by trained parents. Local support groups.*

Parents Anonymous
6-9 Manor Gardens
London N7 6LA
(071) 263 8918
Telephone helpline run by volunteers for parents under stress who feel they can't cope or might abuse their children.

LOSS AND BEREAVEMENT

(See also 'Child' under 'Support and information'.)

Foundation for the Study of Infant Deaths (Cot Death Research and Support)
(E, W & NI)
35 Belgrave Square
London SW1X 8Q8
(071) 235 0965
Support and information for parents bereaved by a sudden infant death and support with any subsequent babies. Can put parents in touch with local support groups of other parents who have also suffered bereavement. Produce infant care guidance card including symptoms of serious illness to watch out for in babies.*
In Northern Ireland:
Friends of the Foundation for the Study of Infant Deaths
7 Glennan Avenue
Belfast BT17 9HT
(0232) 622688

Miscarriage Association
c/o Clayton Hospital
Northgate
Wakefield
W. Yorks WF1 3JS
(0924) 200799
Information, advice and support for women who have had, or who are having, a miscarriage. Local contacts and groups.*

SAFTA (Support after Termination for Abnormality)
(E, W & NI)
29 Soho Square
London W1V 6JB
(071) 439 6124
Self-help charity offering support and information to parents who have had a termination because an abnormality was diagnosed in their baby. Support given by parents who have undergone a similar experience.*

Scottish Cot Death Trust
Royal Hospital for Sick Children
Yorkhill
Glasgow G3 8SJ
(041) 357 3946
Support and information for parents bereaved by sudden infant death. Puts parents in touch with local support groups of other bereaved parents.*

Stillbirth and Neonatal Death Society (SANDS)
28 Portland Place
London W1N 4DE
(071) 436 5881
Information and a national network of support groups for bereaved parents.*

ILLNESS AND DISABILITY

BLISS
17-21 Emerald Street
London WC1N 3QL
(071) 831 9393
Parent support network providing emotional and practical support to the families of babies who need intensive or special care. Local groups.*

Contact a Family
16 Strutton Ground
London SW1P 2HP
(071) 222 2695
National charity offering information, advice and support to parents of children with special needs and disabilities. Links parents to local support groups for general support or to nationally run groups or, in the case of rare disorders, to individuals in similar circumstances.*

Disabled Living Centre
Musgrave Park Hospital
Stockman's Lane
Belfast BT9 7JB
Information and advice on all aspects of disability, especially equipment and dealing with living problems. Referral to other organisations for adults and children with disabilities.

Disability Action
22 Annadale Avenue
Belfast BT7 3UR
(0232) 491011
Provides information and advice on physical disability and local organisations.

Disability Information Trust
Mary Marlborough Lodge
Nuffield Orthopaedic Centre
Headington
Oxford OX3 7LD
(0865) 750103
Assesses and tests equipment for people with disabilities. Publishes information in series 'Equipment for Disabled People'.*

Genetic Interest Group (GIG)
c/o Institute of Molecular Medicine
John Radcliffe Hospital
Oxford OX3 9DU
(0865) 744002
Organisation which aims to promote understanding and awareness of genetic diseases. If you're concerned about the risk of genetic disease to you or your family, they will refer you to appropriate organisations such as a regional genetic centre or self-help group.*

National Association for the Welfare of Children in Hospital
(NAWCH) (E)
Argyle House
29-31 Euston Road
London NW1 2SD
(071) 833 2041
In Scotland:
Action for Sick Children (Scotland)
15 Smith Place
Edinburgh EH6 8HT
(031) 553 6553
In Wales:
Association for the Welfare of Children in Hospital (AWCH)
2 Chestnut Avenue
West Cross
Swansea SA3 5NL
(0792) 404232
In Northern Ireland:
AWCH
c/o Mrs Jones
Bryson House
Bedford Street
Belfast BT2 7FE
(0232) 799215 (after 6 pm)
Advice and support for families with sick children. Helps them make use of the health service. Telephone advice. There may be a local group you can join.*

Voluntary Council for Handicapped Children
8 Wakley Street
London EC1V 7QE
(071) 278 9441
Information for parents and details of organisations offering help with particular disabilities.*

SPECIALISED ORGANISATIONS

Association for Spina Bifida and Hydrocephalus (ASBAH) (E & W)
ASBAH House
42 Park Road
Peterborough PE1 2UQ
(0733) 555988
In Scotland:
Scottish Spina Bifida Association
190 Queensferry Road
Edinburgh EH4 2BW
(031) 332 0743

In Northern Ireland:
Northern Ireland Spina Bifida and Hydrocephalus Association
3rd Floor
Bryson House
28 Bedford Street
Belfast BT2 7FE
(0232) 333838
Information, advice, counselling and support for parents. Local support groups.*

Cleft Lip and Palate Association (CLAPA)
1 Eastwood Gardens
Kenton
Newcastle-upon-Tyne
NE3 3DQ
(091) 285 9396
Voluntary organsiation of parents and professionals offering support to families of babies born with cleft lip and/or palate. Feeding equipment available. Local groups.*

Cystic Fibrosis Research Trust
Alexandra House
5 Blyth Road
Bromley BR1 3RS
(081) 464 7211
In Northern Ireland:
Cystic Fibrosis Research Trust in Northern Ireland
1 Circular Road East
Cultra
Co Down BT18 0HA
(0232) 425982
In Wales:
Cystic Fibrosis Research Trust in Wales
18 Pine Tree Close
Radyr
Cardiff CF4 8RQ
(0222) 843394
In Scotland:
Cystic Fibrosis Research Trust in Scotland
Inverallan
26 West Argyle Street
Helensburgh
Dunbartonshire G84 8DB
(0436) 76791
Informtion and support for parntns of children with cystic fibrosis and for people worried about the possibility of passing on the illness. Local groups.*

Down's Syndrome Association (E & W)
155 Mitcham Road
Tooting
London SW17 9PG
(081) 682 4001
In Scotland:
Scottish Down's Syndrome Association
158-160 Balgreen Road
Edinburgh EH11 3AU
(031)313 4225
In Northern Ireland:
Down's Syndrome Association
3rd Floor
Bryson House
28 Bedford Street
Belfast BT2 7FE
(0232) 243266
Information, advice, counselling and support for parent's of children with Down's Syndrome. Local groups. 24-hour helpline.*

Haemophilia Society
123 Westminster Bridge Road
London SE1 7HR
(071) 928 2020
Information, advice and practical help for families affected by haemophilia. Some local groups.*
In Northern Ireland:
67 Woodvale Road
Belfast BT13 3BM

Heart Care Children's Heart Support Federation
112 Irish Street
Downpatrick
Co Down BT30 6PT
(0396) 641206
National charity which will put

parents of children born with heart problems in touch with local parent support groups throughout the UK 24-hour telephone help.

Jennifer Trust for Spinal Muscular Atrophy
11 Ash Tree Close
Wellesbourne
Warwickshire CV35 9SA
(0789) 842377
Self-help group offering information and support to parents of children with the disease. Can put you in touch with other parents. Equipment on loan.*

MENCAP (Royal Society for Mentally Handicapped Children and Adults) (E, W & NI)
MENCAP National Centre
123 Golden Lane
London EC1Y 0RT
(071) 454 0454
In Scotland:
Scottish Society for the Mentally Handicapped
13 Elmbank Street
Glasgow G2 4QA
(041) 226 4541
In Northern Ireland:
MENCAP in Northern Ireland
4 Annadale Avenue
Belfast BT7 3JH
(0232) 691351
Information, support and advice for parents of children with mental handicap. Local groups.*

Meningitis Research
Old Gloucester Road
Alverston
Bristol BS12 2LQ
(0454) 413344
In Northern Ireland:
29 Springwell Street
Ballymena BT43 6AJ
(0266) 652060
Offers counselling for parents whose children have died from meningitis and gives support to people with loved ones in hospital or at home. A 24-hour national helpline is available: (0454) 413344.*

Muscular Dystrophy Group of Great Britain and Northern Ireland
35 Macaulay Road
London SW4 0QP
(071) 720 8055
Information, advice and support for families affected by muscular dystrophy.*

National Society for Phenylketonuria and Allied Disorders
7 Southfield Close
Willen
Milton Keynes MK15 9LL
(0908) 691653
Self-help organisation offering information and support to families affected by the disorder. Newsletter.*

Northern Ireland Council for Orthopaedic Development
2nd floor
Scottish Provident Building
7 Donegall Square West
Belfast BT1 6JD
(0232) 328378
Offers advice and support to parents of children with cerebral palsy.

REACH (The Association for Children with Hand or Arm Deficiency)
13 Park Terrace
Crimchard
Chard
Somerset TA20 1LA
(0460) 61578
Information and support to parents of children with hand or arm problems. Can put you in touch with individual families in a similar situation or local groups.*

SENSE (National Deaf-Blind and Rubella Association)
11-13 Clifton Terrace
London N4 3SR
(071) 272 7774
Information, advice and support for families of deaf-blind and rubella handicapped children.*
In Northern Ireland:
Wilton House
5 College Square North
Belfast BT1 6AR
(0232) 439961

Sickle Cell Society
54 Station Road
Harlesden
London NW10 4UA
(081) 961 7795/8346
Information, advice and counselling on sickle cell disease and trait.*

Society for Mucopolysaccharide Disorders
7 Chessfield Park
Little Chalfont
Bucks HP6 6RU
(0494) 762789
Information and support to families of children affected by this and related disorders. Local groups.*

The Spastics Society
12 Park Crescent
London W1N 4EQ
(071) 636 5020
Offers advice and support to parents of children with cerebral palsy.*

Tay Sachs and Allied Diseases Association
c/o Royal Manchester Children's Hospital
Pendlebury
Manchester M27 1HA
(061) 794 4696 ex 2384 answerphone
Information, counselling and practical support to families affected by these disorders.*

Toxoplasmosis Trust
Room 26
61-71 Collier Street
London N1 9BE
(071) 713 0663
Information, advice and counselling for pregnant women with toxoplasmosis, parents of infected children and others with toxoplasmosis.*

The UK Thalassaemia Society
107 Nightingale Lane
London N8 7QY
(081) 348 0437
Information, advice and support for families affected by thalassaemia and for possible carriers.*

CHILDCARE

Daycare Trust/National Childcare Campaign
Wesley House
4 Wild Court
London WC2B 5AU
(071) 405 5617/8
Information and advice on obtaining suitable forms of childcare and on setting up daycare.*

National Childminding Association (E & W)
8 Masons Hill
Bromley BR2 9EY
(081) 464 6164
In Scotland:
Scottish Childminding Association
Room 15
Stirling Business Centre
Wellgreen
Stirling ST8 2DZ
(0786) 445377
In Northern Ireland:
Northern Ireland Childminding Association
17A Court Street

Newtownards
Co Down BT23 5NX
(0247) 811015
Associations for childminders, childcare workers, parents and others with an interest in daycare and who wish to improve the standards of day care.*

Northern Ireland Pre-school Playgroups Association (NIPPA)
Unit 3
Enterprise House
Boucher Crescent
Belfast BT12 6HU
(0232) 662825
A voluntary association of mother and toddler groups, playgroups and families of the under 5's who attend them. Provides help and support through a network covering Northern Ireland.

Working for Childcare
77 Holloway Road
London N7 8JZ
(071) 700 0281
Advice and information for employers, trade unions and parents on developing childcare at work.*

FAMILY PLANNING

Family Planning Association
27/35 Mortimer Street
London W1N 7RJ
(071) 636 7866
In Northern Ireland:
113 University Street
Belfast BT7 1HP
(0232) 325488
In Wales:
4 Museum Place
Cardiff CF1 3BG
(0222) 644034
Information on all aspects of family planning and methods of contraception.*

Family Planning Brook Advisory Centres (E, S & NI)
Brook Central Office
153A East Street
London SE17 2SD
(071) 708 1234
Advice and practical help with contraception and pregnancy testing, advice on unplanned pregnancies and sexual counselling for young men and women. Free and confidential. For your nearest centre look in the local phone book or contact Brook Central Office.*

Marie Stopes Clinic
Marie Stopes House
108 Whitfield Street
London W1P 6BE
(071) 388 0662
Registered charity providing family planning, women's health check-ups, male and female sterilisation, pregnancy testing, advide on unplanned pregnancies and sexual counselling for men and women. You don't need to be referred by your doctor, but you need to book an appointment. A charge is made to cover costs. For centres in Manchester and Leeds look in the local phone book*

ALCOHOL

Alcohol Concern (E & W)
275 Gray's Inn Road
London WC1X 8QF
(071) 833 3471
In Wales:
Alcohol Concern Wales
Ground Floor
4 Dock Chambers
Bute Street
Cardiff CF1 6AG
In Scotland:
Scottish Council on Alcohol
137-145 Sauchiehall Street
Glasgow G2 3EW

(041) 333 9677
In Northern Ireland:
Council on Alcohol
40 Elmwood Avenue
Belfast BT9 6AZ
(0232) 664434
Information on alcohol problems, what types of services exist and where you can get help locally.*

Alcoholics Anonymous (AA) (E, S & W)
AA General Service Office
PO Box 1
Stonebow House
Stonebow
York YO1 2NJ
(0904) 644026
Network of independent self-help groups whose members encourage each other to stop drinking and to stay off drink. First names only are used to preserve anonymity. For your nearest group look in the phone book or contact the AA General Service Office*.

Dunlewy Substance Advice Centre
1A Dunlewy Street
Belfast BT13 2QU
(0232) 324197
Offers help and personal counselling on alcohol, drug and solvent abuse.

Northern Ireland Council on Alcohol (NICA)
40 Elmwood Avenue
Belfast BT9 6AZ
(0232) 664434
Provides counselling, treatment, education, information and training or dealing with alcohol problems.

Northlands
13 Pump Street
Londonderry
(0504) 263356
Gives advice, information and counselling for those with alcohol or other drug related problems.

SMOKING

Smokers' Quitline
(071) 487 3000
Advice on stopping smoking and details of local stop smoking support services. Phone between 9.30 am and 5.30 pm on weekdays. Recorded advice available at other times. If you prefer to write for information:

Quit*
102 Gloucester Place
London W1H 3DA

Ulster Cancer Foundation
40-42 Eglantine Avenue
Belfast BR9 6DX
(0232) 663281/2/3
Carries out cancer research and education programmes in Northern Ireland. Also provides information on the dangers of smoking and provides advice and support to smokers who want to quit.

ADDICTIVE DRUGS

(See also 'Dunlewy Substance Advice Centre' and 'Northlands' under 'Alcohol')

Drugaid Cardiff (W)
1 Neville Street
Cardiff CF1 8LP
Meeting every Wednesday from 6.30 pm to 9 pm. If you need advice outside of meetings, contact All Wales Drugsline on freephone 0800 220794.

Narcotics Anonymous
PO Box 417
London SW10 0DP

(071) 498 9005
Self-help organisations whose members help each other to stay clear of drugs. Write or phone between 12 pm and 8 pm for information and the address of your local group. Some groups have a crèche.*

SCODA (The Standing Conference on Drug Abuse) (E, NI & W)
1-4 Hatton Place
London EC1N 8ND
(071) 430 2341
In Scotland:
Scottish Drug Forum
5 Oswald Street
Glasgow G1 4QR
(041) 221 1175
Information on local treatment and services for drug users, family and friends.*

For England you can also ask the operator for Freefone Drug Problems which will give you a contact number for your local area. In Wales you can phone All Wales Drugsline on free-phone 0800 220794.

HIV AND AIDS

National AIDS Helpline
0800 567123
Calls are confidential, free and available 24 hours a day. There is a Minicom on 0800 521361 for people who are deaf or hard of hearing. Information in other languages: Bengali, Gujerati, Hindi, Punjabi, Urdu and English on Wednesday 6 pm – 10 pm on 0800 282445. Cantonese and English on Tuesdays 6 pm – 10 pm on 0800 282446. Arabic and English on Wednesdays 6 pm – 10 pm on 0800 282447. Leaflets can be ordered in all these languages.*

Positively Women
5 Sebastian Street
London EC1V 0HE
(071) 490 5515
Information and practical and emotional support for women with a positive HIV diagnosis or who have ARC or AIDS, including women who are pregnant or who have children. Support group.*

SUPPORT FOR STRESS OR DEPRESSION

Association for Post-Natal Illness (APNI)
25 Jerdan Place
London SW6 1BE
(071) 386 0868
Network of telephone and postal volunteers who have suffered from postnatal illness and offer information, support and encouragement on a one-to-one basis.*

CRY-SIS Support Group
BM CRY-SIS
London WC1N 3XX
(071) 404 5011
Help and support for parents of babies who cry excessively or who have a sleep problem.

Parents Advice Centre (NI)
Room 1 Bryson House
28 Bedford Street
Belfast BT2 7FE
(0232) 238800
A 24-hour confidential service offering support and guidance to parents under stress.

INDEX